successful business woman

Janet Macdonald is an accountant by profession and a business woman by inclination. She received her education at grammar school and technical colleges. Her career has brought her into contact with many businesses both large and small, and she currently works for an international banking group.

In addition, she ran for many years a specialised riding equipment business. She started the Ladies' Side-Saddle Association in 1974 and held the chair for six years, during which she travelled extensively to lecture and train other teachers.

She lives in Croydon with an investment consultant and a black cat, but hopes soon to move out into the country.

'This is an easy-to-read guide packed with useful tips.'

Accountancy Age

by the same author

Riding Side-Saddle (*with Val Francis*)
Running a Stables as a Business
The Right Horse: An Owners' and Buyers' Guide
Running a Tack-Shop as a Business
Climbing the Ladder: How to be a Woman Manager

JANET W. MACDONALD

How to be a successful business woman

Working for yourself

A Methuen Paperback

A Methuen Paperback

First published in Great Britain 1987
by Methuen London Ltd
11 New Fetter Lane, London EC4P 4EE
© 1987 Janet W. Macdonald

Printed in Great Britain by
Cox and Wyman Ltd, Reading

British Library Cataloguing in Publication Data

Macdonald, Janet W.
    How to be a successful business woman:
    working for yourself.
    1. Success in business   2. Women in
    business
    I. Title
    650.1'024042   HF5386

ISBN 0–413–15570–6

This book is sold subject to the condition that it shall
not, by way of trade or otherwise, be lent, resold,
hired out, or otherwise circulated without the pub-
lisher's prior consent in any form of binding or cover
other than that in which it is published and without a
similar condition including this condition being im-
posed on the subsequent purchaser.

For Dawn Dodd-Noble

who is the most successful and astute business woman I know

Contents

Introduction

There must be as many definitions of success as there are reasons for running your own business. At its very least, success is keeping the business running – in itself no mean feat, since something like 90 per cent of new businesses fail within their first year. At the other end of the scale is a Stock Exchange listing, fame and fortune and all the trappings that the modern world sees as success.

Whatever your personal ambitions, I do not feel you can consider yourself a successful businesswoman unless you are making more money than you would by putting the same amount of time and effort into working for someone else. You should also be making more from your capital than you would by investing that money in any other medium.

Make no mistake – running a business is something you do to make money and to do that you have to be money-orientated. You have to be able to do sums and calculate percentages and profits in your head quickly and accurately. You have to keep an eye to the main chance, and learn to view all situations from a 'What's in it for him, what's in it for me?' standpoint; and you have to watch the pennies coming in and going out, all the time. If you are not prepared to spend that much time and attention on your money, or you don't think it matters, you shouldn't be in business for yourself – and you won't be for long, for that way lies failure.

Nor should you start your own business because you are fed up with having to do what you are told by your employer, or tired of the constant hassle of office politics.

Running a business is full of hassle, from suppliers, customers, staff, officialdom and competitors.

All this, of course, is perfectly valid for men, too, so why write a book just for women? The fact of the matter is that many of us cling to attitudes that serve us badly in the dynamic cut-throat world of business. We are just not in the habit of thinking and reacting as we should in a business situation. Most of us have been brought up to be thoughtful and kind and honest, and it never occurs to us that all the people we meet are not the same. We do not realise that the business people we meet (and especially chauvinistic business men) have as their prime objective the furtherance of their own business. We expect them to go out of their way to help us for no reward and then we do not understand why they don't; or worse, we go out of our way to do things for other people when we should be devoting our efforts to our business.

In a small book like this one cannot go too deeply into specific businesses, but the general principles are the same for all, and the jackals wait for the unwary in every field.

I have assumed that you will be starting in business on your own, or as the principal in a small business.

August 1986

1 What business?

It may seem silly to state that your choice of business is crucial to your chances of success, but the wrong decision could mean you are doomed to failure from the beginning. Not only is the decision on what business to run crucial, but so is your perception of exactly what that business is. The classic example of this is the linoleum manufacturers who were in deep trouble until someone pointed out that what they actually made was floor coverings and it was time they started to produce some in modern materials and designs. So while discussing some of the areas you might consider, I have tried to pinpoint what those businesses are really about.

Incidentally, if you are convinced you want to go into business on your own, but don't know what you want to do, beware of advertisements for books and magazines offering 'business opportunities'. Rather like people who sell 'infallible' methods of winning the football pools, one should wonder why, if they are so clever, they aren't using them themselves. Such magazines, while they may have some good ideas, are very expensive, make you take out at least one year's subscription, and their prime purpose is to make money for the publishers.

Any averagely intelligent woman who keeps her eyes and ears open as she goes about her daily life should see plenty of business opportunities. A couple of examples to illustrate this are the woman who noticed young mothers struggling home with bulky packets of disposable nappies, and now runs a thriving baby goods home-delivery service; or the woman who listened to a group of friends discussing their anxieties about getting themselves or their children home late at night, and started a women's taxi service exclusively driven by women.

There are probably more business openings in the female sector now than there have ever been, and they are growing as more women have well-paid jobs and thus more disposable income. Many of these women need help with their homes and their lifestyles. The openings here are for wardrobe engineering, house-cleaning, decorating and renovation, catering, and child-care. The first three are available as franchises (of which more later) but there is nothing to stop you going it alone.

Wardrobe engineering requires you to have a flair for fashion and an in-depth knowledge of where to buy specific items. You interview the client to establish her lifestyle, needs and taste, then inspect her existing wardrobe, show her how to enhance the good items and encourage her to throw away the others. You advise on colours, accessories and make-up and then either bring her a selection of items to choose from or accompany her on shopping expeditions. As well as a fee from the client, you should receive commission from shops and dressmakers. In addition to a deep interest in clothes, you need a great deal of tact and patience and you should be prepared to listen to a lot of stories about unhappy love affairs, for you can easily become a convenient ear for your clients to unburden themselves.

Where house-cleaning is concerned, there are two options. Either you run an employment agency specialising in cleaning staff (more on employment agencies later) on a permanent or 'temp' basis, or you organise teams of people who descend on the client's home. With the latter, you offer a range of set jobs, from 'the complete springclean with carpets and curtains cleaned' to 'dust, hoover and make beds' and you have set prices for each job dependant on the size and number of rooms. You will need a smart van to transport staff and equipment, considerable knowledge of how to deal with rare or delicate items and a willingness to pitch in with a hoover when staff are ill. You could expand your service to do office cleaning as well.

You may be able to combine this with decoration and renovation, which also requires teams of workers as well as your own design ability. Obviously the workers need to be painters and decorators rather than dusters and ironers, but the principles of running a team are the same.

For a straightforward decorating job, you interview the client, agree a colour scheme and show her samples of paper and fabrics; then your team moves in and does the decorating work while another team or a local contact makes curtains and upholstery. You get a fee for the consultancy and the work, and commission or discount on materials. For more radical renovations or alterations, you will need to produce drawings and colour boards for the client to approve; then deal with planning authorities and builders as well as your own decorating team. You could combine either of these with franchises for fitted kitchens, bathrooms, bedrooms, etc.

Child-care services also come in several varieties. You could run a nursery or day-school, but these are hedged round with regulations and restrictions and are not very profitable. Better perhaps to go the agency route, dealing with nannies, au pairs, baby-sitters or something like the famous 'Universal Aunts' who will do anything from meeting a child at school to taking it to the zoo. This latter service has great scope for working mothers who may not want a permanent helper, but need someone to deal with visits to the dentist.

Working women are also the ones most likely to need help with home catering. Whether it is cooking to stock a freezer, a children's party or a large formal dinner party, the basic decisions are 'Your kitchen or mine, your utensils or mine, your ingredients or mine?' If it's your kitchen you will be working on familiar ground but may be distracted by family demands. (It would also be reasonable for a client to ask to see your kitchen to judge your standards of hygiene.) If it's your utensils and serving dishes, you will have to go back to collect them, unless you also stay to serve and wash up. If it's your ingredients you can buy wholesale and make a little extra on them.

Catering is often the first area women think of when contemplating their own business, but it is one that is fraught with problems, and one that has the reputation of being the quickest route to bankruptcy. You don't risk much by doing home or office catering; nor is there any more risk in food manufacturing than there is in any other form of manufacturing (assuming that you stick to the rules on hygiene). The real risk area is catering to the public, whether it be a tea shop, wine bar or fully fledged restaurant. The problem is that unless you have considerable experience of working in (and preferably actually managing) one of these places, you tend to think that a love of food and cooking is what counts. It isn't – what counts is rigid portion control, shrewd buying and costing, constant attention to detail and a willingness to work long unsociable hours dealing with temperamental staff and customers.

Staying on the theme of providing goods and services for women, but not necessarily working women, there are the perennials of health, beauty and fashion.

All three areas offer retail opportunities and the first two can also be run on a club or hydro basis. You do not necessarily need great technical expertise in either case, as long as you have access to competent staff who will provide beauty treatments, massage and exercise routines, or qualified medical staff if you go for a health farm. The latter are run on a hotel basis and require a great deal of capital and a carefully chosen location. There are probably few openings in this area, but there is scope in every town for a locally appropriate variation on the hairdresser/beauty salon/dance studio/exercise club theme. Apart from the obvious services, there are many lucrative sidelines available here, from sunbed hire to retail sales of cosmetics or leotards.

One area of health and beauty that is enjoying a boom at the moment is that of natural products. You might like to consider health foods, organic market gardening, herbs, or natural and non-cruelty tested beauty products. The most successful of these are the famous Body Shop franchises, but there is still scope for others.

Is your heart set on a dress-shop or boutique? Think again, very carefully, before you commit yourself. While they can be very profitable, the best chance of success is not in the high fashion areas but in everyday clothes for everyday people. There, providing you can compete with the chain stores, you are less at the mercy of rapidly changing trends or our fickle climate, either of which can leave you with expensive unmovable stock.

A low-risk but quite lucrative way to dip your toe in the clothing water is the currently popular used-clothing agency. Here you have no outlay on stock, for you charge a commission on the items brought for you to sell, but you must still provide inviting premises and an air of confidentiality. If you get these right you will soon build up a regular clientele, but you have to be very picky about both the style and the condition of the items you accept for sale.

Another of the classic ways to lose your life savings is to open a gift shop. This is also a fashion business (so are toys) with all the attendant risks of short-lived fads, and it is also a very seasonal business with more than half of its trade done in the three months before Christmas. Get your buying wrong, and you will find yourself in January with a load of stock that won't shift until next October, unless you are able to cart it off to a tourist area for the summer season.

Apropos of taking your stock somewhere else in the summer, one way of doing this is to have a show stand which you take to county shows, exhibitions and so on. Some businesses do nothing else and thrive, but don't assume that it is an easy or cheap way of retailing. You need an expensive permanent show unit, a method of moving it and your living accommodation from place to place, and a taste for the nomadic life. It can be tremendous fun, for you will find the same stand-holders and the same competitors at almost every show on the summer circuit, and lots of personable men on the loose from home, if that is your taste.

On the other hand, given inclement weather, outdoor events can be cold, wet and muddy (and your stock will soon get that way too); it is always hard work; thieves abound and site rents are not cheap. Do not forget that the object of the exercise, as far as the organisers are concerned, is to make money for themselves. It costs several hundred pounds a day for the smallest site at any decent show or exhibition, and the major exhibition centres are heavily unionised, so woe betide you if you are foolish enough to pick up a hammer.

If you have a taste for retailing, you need, as well as all the normal considerations of location, size and market-slot, to give some thought to the physical proportions of your stock. Unless you have a tame man or a taste for body-building, you would be wise to avoid items that require brute strength to handle. Even the innocent paperback book is heavy when it comes in boxes of fifty, and delivery men won't even stack boxes in your store-room, let alone carry them from there to the shelves. Working in a shop is tiring enough without the insidious nag of a damaged back.

You wouldn't think of running a shop without having worked in one for a while, would you? Amazing though it may seem, people do, only to give up after a few months when they've found out that there's more to it than opening the door at nine, shutting it at five-thirty, and taking money in between. Apart from all the normal paperwork and physically keeping the shelves full, you have to give constant thought to what is or isn't selling, and what you will sell in the future. If you are dealing with anything specialised, you may have problems obtaining supplies, may have to go to trade fairs abroad to keep up with trends, and if you buy foreign goods direct from the manufacturers you may have problems enforcing quality control. I know the trade fairs sound like fun, but it will be expensive fun, and you will need to speak the language very well indeed if you are not to be taken advantage of.

That said, if you can tolerate the Great British Public, if you can stay half a jump ahead of trends, and if you can get your prices right, there is a lot of money to be made in shops.

You don't even have to start from scratch, for there is a thriving trade in shops of all kinds. Look for them in *Exchange and Mart, Daltons Weekly* or the *London Weekly Advertiser* (for London and the Home Counties) or go to a business transfer agent (find them in the *Yellow Pages*) and explain what you want. They will have a list of likely businesses or properties and they will also provide stock auditors, offer to help you raise money and help in other ways if you are inclined to let them. Just keep in mind the fact that they gain their main fee from the vendors, as do estate agents, and be sure there can be no conflict of interest between that and the services they offer you.

If you do buy an existing shop business (or any other business for that matter) you will need to have copies of the accounts for at least the last four years to get them checked out by your accountant. The accounts may well tell a different story on takings from the verbal one you've been told with a nudge and a wink, but even if this is the case, you should still base your price offer on what the accounts say. If the owner has been systematically fiddling the Inland Revenue and the VAT man, he can't expect to get the benefit of the true takings at sale time as well as the benefit of undeclared income.

Incidentally, when I refer to what the accounts 'say', I mean what they really say, not what they have been doctored to say. A clever accountant can 'massage' the figures to paint a rosy picture in a number of ways, and it needs an equally clever accountant to read between the lines and spot it. The classic trick is to show turnover increasing dramatically in the last few years, but this can be done by juggling stock valuations or actually dropping prices to an unprofitable level to boost sales. Even if sales are genuinely high, take the trouble to find out the reason. I know of one man who bought an off-licence a few months before the local brewery went on a prolonged strike. They were out for over a year, and it did wonders for his sales over two trading years, as he was the only source of beer in the area. The brewery resumed work and he sold his business for an enormous profit and went to Spain where the unfortunate buyer couldn't get at him. Moral – don't just look at the official accounts, look at all the working books as well, and if there is a sudden surge in the takings, investigate local history.

You should do this anyway. Unless the vendor says he is retiring and produces his pension plans to prove it, you shouldn't take too much notice of his stated reasons for selling, unless this will have a bearing on the price or method of payment. He may even find it tax-advantageous to accept payment over a period of time and it is always worth enquiring about this.

And don't let anyone kid you that they are doing you a favour because you have a pretty face. The only favour the vendor of a business is doing is to his bank balance. The more they try to pressurise you into fast decisions, the more suspicious you should be. If they tell you that other buyers are interested, ask detailed questions to see if they exist, like 'Have they made a firm offer?' and 'Have they got the money available or are they still looking for finance?' If you find the answers less than believable, tell them, 'What a pity – but never mind, I've got some other places to look at,' and wait for them to get back to you to say the deal has fallen through and are you still interested?

Don't let them add in a big sum for 'goodwill' either. If there is any genuine goodwill attached to the old pro-prietor, it'll go with him anyway, and you'll have to start from scratch. But on the whole it doesn't matter, as most of the customers will stay with you for a while from inertia. There is only one true price for any business, and that is the one you are prepared to pay. And you can't decide on that until you know exactly what you are getting, which includes tangible assets as well as future potential. Do be sure the vendor details everything and proves title to it, before you go away to do your sums.

One final point, which concerns employees. If there are some attached to the business and you don't want them, make sure this is made clear in the contract or you may find you are lumbered with getting rid of them and finding their severance pay.

There are of course other types of business which might interest you. One of the first thoughts to come to women who have worked in offices is to provide secretarial services. The usual routine is to start off by doing the work yourself at home and farming out what you cannot cope with when demand grows. If you do it this way you must be very firm about the quality of the work and you must not let your home-workers have any direct contact with the client or you could lose both, to their mutual advantage and the detriment of your profits.

You will inevitably need some expensive office equipment (typewriters and photocopiers at the very least) and somewhere to operate them. You may prefer to have the work done on your premises to save all the delivery and collection of work to or by your home-workers, which means even bigger premises. One of our local bureaux combines this work with a secretarial training college, using senior students for a lot of the work.

The logical next step from this is a fully fledged employment agency, but it is not a sensible step for the uninitiated. Not only do you have to spend a high proportion of your time on the telephone trying to convince local businesses that your staff are better than the competition's (and there is so much competition that the recipients of your calls are more likely to brush you off than listen), you also have to comply with the Employment Agencies Act.

Before you can do anything you must have a licence, which involves a very detailed application form and displaying notices on the proposed premises and in the local paper in case of objections. Once you have your licence, you have to do a great deal of paperwork and book-keeping in a prescribed form. You have to know your employment law thoroughly and you have the responsibility of checking that your job candidates have any qualifications required by law for the job.

You are not allowed to charge job-seekers, and it may be

some time before the new employer pays you, especially if the candidate has to give three months' notice from a current job. If the candidate turns out to be a dud, the employer will expect a refund. If this happens too often, the word will go out on the grapevine, so you need an ability to judge candidates for suitability and work-enthusiasm. If you are providing temps, there will also be a time lag between your paying them at the end of the week and your client paying your invoice. Whichever way you operate, you will need enough working capital to support the business until the fees start rolling in.

One last specific area I will offer for your consideration is that of selling financial services. While much of it involves life assurance, don't deride it for that. I know it has had a bad image in the past, but there are some pretty dreadful solicitors and accountants about too.

Financial services tend to involve life assurance because it is often the best answer to a complex tax situation, because it is a good way to save (the companies mostly have a good record of investment management) and because any lender of money wants a life policy on the borrower. You can specialise in business loans (see Chapter Two), school fees, investment, pensions or tax mitigation, and if you are good at it the financial world is your oyster.

The way it works is that you join either a big specialist insurance broker or the selling arm of a unit-linked life assurance company as a self-employed agent. They pay you commission on the sales you make and provide training, office accommodation and technical expertise. You can earn a lot of money if you work hard and are not restricted to the profits of your own sales, for they are always anxious to encourage the development of team leaders who receive bonuses on team results. Right now, the scope for this opportunity is enormous for there are few women doing it, and there are many female clients who would rather deal with another woman.

On a more generalised note, another alternative is to go into consultancy on a freelance basis. Whether you stay on your own or link up with some like-minded colleagues is up to you, but obviously you should not be venturing into areas where you have no track record. Whatever your field, you will need considerable expertise and experience covering several work situations if you are to be credible. Many successful consultants were pushed into it by redundancy, but even if this is not the case you may find your current and past employers willing to help. They'd all rather deal with a known quantity. You did do a good job for them, didn't you?

One of the areas where there is still scope for consultants is data-processing, which serves to illustrate an important point. Do be sure that your chosen field is expanding, or you will soon find yourself broke and back at the employment agencies. There is no point in being the world expert on buggy whips when everybody is driving a car.

It is generally considered that the dependable growth areas are electronics, high technology and communications, in both commerce and the home, and anything connected with the leisure industry, from holidays to food, health, beauty, education, music, sport and entertainment. Plenty of choice there, and plenty of entrepreneurs who would like a slice of the action if only they could find someone to tell them how to go about it.

If you would prefer someone to tell you in detail how to go about things on an ongoing basis, you might consider taking up a franchise. There are an enormous variety available now, from women-oriented areas (Pronuptia – bridal clothes; Poppies – house-cleaning; Body Shops – natural beauty products; Colour Counsellors – house decoration;

etc., etc.) through generalised areas (fast food, health food, driving schools, etc., etc.) to areas normally considered male preserves (printing, drain-clearing, car-tuning, etc.) You pays your money and you takes your choice, but you would be wise to check out the deal you are being offered very carefully, especially if the franchisor is not a member of the British Franchise Association, for this area is as prone as any other to the cowboy operators who see a chance of separating the inexperienced from their money.

The basic principle with franchises is that you pay the franchisor for the right to use his trade name and proven business format. Since he does not want his good name damaged, he retains the right to dictate how you run the business, often in very fine detail. Fast food outlets insist on rigid portion control and rigid adherence to recipes (most make you buy supplies from them); all insist on standard décor and many insist on a particular style of record-keeping.

In return you get training and advice, the benefit of national advertising, and help in raising finance. Lenders of money welcome potential franchisees with open arms, for they know that your new venture is much more likely to succeed than if you go it alone. (The percentage rate is about the same in both cases – 90 per cent of new franchises *do* succeed, 90 per cent of other new ventures *don't!*)

Actually, the first hint of danger with the cowboys is often an inability (or unwillingness) to introduce you to potential lenders, for they do not want any sort of come-back. Another danger signal is a big start-up fee and low royalties, for they may not intend to stay around to bother to collect these. Alternatively, they may be getting a cut from the suppliers of extortionately priced basic materials, having tied you to using that supplier.

Whoever you buy a franchise from, ask to see the

accounts from other existing outlets in locations similar to yours. Beware the franchisor who won't let you have these, or discourages you from contacting other franchisees, or who gives evasive answers to direct questions like 'What are the normal turnover/stock cost/profit ratios?' If they are genuine, honest, and know their business, they will have such figures immediately available.

Beware also the 'franchise' that is nothing of the sort, but actually the latest version of pyramid selling (now itself illegal). What you buy into is a pyramidical network of 'distributorships' of some obscure product and the idea is that you receive an increasingly large 'override' on the profits of the people below you as you rise through the ranks. I once found myself at a presentation for one of these deals under the guise of a social evening, and immediately spotted the flaw. They briefly showed us the products, which were OK but very expensive compared with the equivalent available in any grocers, but they concentrated on the advantages of building up your team of junior distributors and the fact that they all had to get their supplies through you. Questions on national marketing campaigns, local advertising and how much of which product the average distributor would actually sell and how he went about it were fobbed off with 'You don't *have* to *sell* it, we all have plenty of friends who will buy, it practically sells itelf.'

All of which goes to show that while there are plenty of good viable business opportunities available, there are also a lot of duds. So, don't commit yourself to anything until you, and your bank manager, and your accountant, and your solicitor, are all convinced that it is a good idea.

And don't commit yourself to anything, no matter how good an opportunity, unless you are convinced you will be happy doing it for many years.

2 Money matters

The first essential to starting a business is money – lots of it. Not only do you need to get premises, equipment and maybe stock, you also need enough to pay day-to-day expenses until the takings start to roll in. If you don't have enough money available at the beginning, you will have to borrow it.

This is the point at which beginners say brightly, 'Oh, but I can get some money from the government to start up my business.' I'm sorry to have to disillusion you, but you can't. I know there are many schemes which come and go and change names with each government and its budgets, but they mostly work on a tax credit basis, which is not a lot of help when you haven't got to the stage of making enough profit for taxes to be due anyway.

There are also the 'enterprise zones' where you can get cheap accommodation and maybe cheap labour, but these are usually depressed areas, so all you can do in them is manufacture goods to be sold elsewhere. (Anything else requires that the locals have spare cash to spend in your business!) What you must understand is that the object of all these schemes is to provide jobs and reduce the unemployment queues, not to encourage small entrepreneurs to set up shops and consultancies which employ no one but the proprietor and perhaps a secretary.*

Some local authorities will provide grants for certain

* There is, at the time of writing, the Enterprise Allowance Scheme, which encourages unemployed people to start up on their own by paying a small weekly amount for up to a year. It does not provide start-up capital, or premises. Details from Job Centres.

types of small business – again usually those which will be providing jobs. Ask for the Industrial Development Officer or the Small Firms Information Service at your local council offices, or ask the Department of Trade and Industry for their Small Firms Service on Freefone 2444. There are many other sources of information on all aspects of running a small business, but I warn you – the whole situation is so fragmented and changes so frequently that quite frankly the best advice I can give is to tell you to approach the local branch of one of the big national firms of accountants. Ask for their expert on small businesses to tell you what is available locally. They will charge you very little, if at all, for a preliminary interview. If you want to do it on your own, get a copy of the BBC's *Small Business Guide* to help you through the maze.

You may be lucky and find an individual who wants to take advantage of the Business Expansion Scheme,* though most invest in institutional schemes. Ask your accountant and solicitor if they know anyone who has some money to spare, wants the BES tax advantages, and is willing to be a 'sleeping partner' (one who has no involvement in the day-to-day running of the business). Or try one of the 'marriage bureaux' that put people with money in touch with people with ideas. If you do find one of these people, they will want a share in the ownership of the business in return for letting you have cheap money.

There is only one source of free money, unless you have a generous rich uncle, and that is a business competition. There are half a dozen of these each year, run by the Design Council, banks, newspapers, development corporations and business-oriented universities. Watch for announce-

---

* Another government scheme that tends to change its name – it was introduced as the 'Business Start-up Scheme' and it offers tax incentives to investors in new companies.

ments in the daily newspapers, especially the *Daily Mail* and the *Daily Express*.

This brings me back to the point I mentioned in the introduction – business is about *money*, and your attitude to it will determine your chances of success. Never forget that it is a commodity and that like any other commodity it has a fluctuating price. That price is dependent on the amount of risk involved in the transaction, as is the availability of the commodity at all.

People starting their first small business are known to be a very bad risk, and none of the companies or organisations that deal in venture capital want to take that risk. They will not lend money (they call it 'seed' capital) to unproven people to start up a business and they do not lend small amounts to anyone. Ask any of them for less than a six-figure sum, and while they will probably be too polite to actually laugh in your face, they will give you the City version of 'Don't call us . . .'

This leaves you with one option only – an ordinary bank. Building societies are not keen to provide money for business loans. Finance houses do, but since they are 'secondary lenders', which means they lend you money they've borrowed themselves, they have to charge you for the interest it costs them as well as for their profit element. Such loans are several percentage points higher than a bank's. Not that a bank will let you have money just like that. Before they even start to look at your business proposition, they will look at you personally and your financial history. For this reason, you should start your search at the bank where you keep your own current account. You do have one, don't you?

If you do, and it has a history of stability, all will be relatively smooth. If you are married and have only a joint account with your husband, or the right to sign cheques on his, you are a very misguided lady and you must change that situation immediately. If you think he won't like it, read the relevant bit of Chapter Nine and talk it over with him – but do it anyway. If you are in the middle of a divorce, talk it over with your solicitor first, in case it will complicate matters, but still do it.

If you are on your own and you do not have a bank account, you are not just misguided, you are a financial imbecile, and any lender will know it and reject you immediately. Even keeping all your money in a building society comes into this category, for they will not give you a bank reference and you must be sure of a good one if you are to be credible to both suppliers and big customers. Both will check you out, you can be sure of that.

It may take a couple of years to build up the sort of credibility you need with your bank manager, but do take the trouble to do it. Use your account regularly, even if you do no more than put the housekeeping in and pay the household bills by cheque. If you have any sort of a lump sum available, put it in one of the bank's high-interest deposit accounts, after an interview with the manager. Ostensibly, it will be to discuss this, but it is actually to let him see your face and for you to get the measure of him. Don't overdraw without prior arrangement (another good excuse to get your face in front of the manager) and don't do anything else silly to make them mark your record card.

Incidentally, when you go to see your bank manager, be careful what you wear. You don't want him to view you as sloppy or as a sex object. So no displays of thigh, midriff or boobs, nor scruffy jeans and sweater. You may think this is irrelevant, but don't forget that people tend to judge you on first impressions and the impression you want to create is that of a mature, sensible business woman. More on the subject of clothes later.

Once the bank manager has accepted you personally as financially responsible, he will then consider you as a business person. Have you ever run this sort of business or any other before, and if so, how successfully? Have you any qualifications? (This won't help much if you have no practical experience to back them up.) How much business acumen do you have? This does not mean you have to be able to read a balance sheet, but you should have prepared a simple cash flow forecast (see page 65) showing expected income and expenses for two or three years. Do be pessimistic about this. One of the major causes of failure in new businesses is shortage of money in the early days. You need to trade for several years to build up goodwill with suppliers, and if you keep them waiting for payment before you have this goodwill, they are liable to panic and sue. Easy access to money buys breathing time.

Next he will consider the business itself. Is it to be a new venture, or are you taking over an existing one? Has it been consistently profitable? He will want proof of this, in the form of copies of the audited accounts for several years. What are the premises like? Have you had them valued? Have you plans and estimates for any improvements? Do you need to buy office equipment? Are you taking over the existing stock? If not, do you also need a stocking loan? He will want to see a priced list of the items you need.

The format of your presentation documents need not be elaborate or formal, but you must not assume that the bank will know anything about the type of business involved. Cover the markets (or customer catchment area if you are thinking of a small shop) and the products, and if you are not to be the sole proprietor give some details about the others, especially their business experience.

At this point, the bank manager will consider your own commitment to the project. He will want to know how much of your own money you are putting into the business, and how much security you can offer for what you borrow. There is no reason why he should lend you money just because you have had what seems to you to be a good idea – all he is interested in is getting the bank's money back on time and getting a proper market return on it in the meantime.

If you want a big chunk of money, and you haven't got some form of solid security, like a house, and you are not going to spend their money buying a property they can have assigned to them, they will want someone who does have some solid worth to guarantee the loan. If you are married, they will ask if your husband is willing. This has nothing to do with your being female, it is just normal business practice to look for someone close to provide the guarantee.

If you only want a few thousand, they might let you have the money with a loan guarantee insurance policy attached, and charge for it with a higher than normal rate of interest. They will also accept life assurance policies as security, providing they are old enough to have a surrender value high enough to cover the loan. (They may even let you do the whole thing on an overdraft basis, but they prefer those to be secured, too.)

Once the proposition has been approved, the period of the loan, interest rate and repayment periods will be set. The loan will almost certainly be for a set period, usually between five and ten years. Repayments will probably be at monthly intervals. The bank then opens a Loan Account for you and transfers the money to your current account, and you are in business. They will be happiest if you sign a standing order for the repayments and woe betide you if that money is not available on time. Two weeks late and they will start writing rude letters – a few more weeks and they will get the deeds to your security out of the vaults and start looking at them with an acquisitive gleam in their eyes!

If your own bank won't lend you the money, ask why not. If the answer is the lame excuse that you want a sum over the manager's limit, or that he has lent his quota for the year, or if he is honest enough to tell you that he doesn't fancy the proposition, you are then at liberty to go to another bank that does. In which case, you will be expected to move all your banking business across.

At this point, rather than start yourself on the long traipse round all the local banks and finance houses, you would do better to enlist the help of a financial expert who does it all the time. By this I mean one of those much maligned people – a life assurance salesman. Don't shy away from the idea – wherever you borrow money, you will have to insure your life as part of the loan agreement. The life salesman's reward for doing the leg-work in finding you the money you need is the commission he earns on the life policy. And you can and should leave it to him. You'll only queer the pitch if you try as well. His local contacts will know that he won't offer them a poor proposition and the fact that he presents it to them is a point in its favour. He will start with his local contacts and move further afield if necessary. He may well know of a bank manager in some other part of the country who is amenable in such cases.

He may suggest a mortgage loan, if you want to buy freehold business premises, which is rather like an ordinary mortgage except that the money comes from institutions like pension funds or insurance company investment funds. He will know if your proposition is likely to find favour with a specialised financial institution, and he will also know whether you might be eligible for the government's Loan Guarantee Scheme. Like all these schemes, this is complex and for certain types of business only – and the rules tend to change with each Budget – but all things being equal the government actually coughs up a substantial chunk of your loan capital to the lender if you can't. It does charge you an extra percentage as 'insurance', but your acceptance under the scheme will gladden the heart of a doubting lender.

Some insurance brokers specialise in this type of business, as do many 'tied' agents. These latter work for the big unit-linked life assurance companies. Find the companies from their advertisements in the Sunday papers, find their local office in the phone book and ask for an appointment with one of their senior agents who specialises in small business loans. If you would prefer to deal with a woman, tell them, or try one of the women listed in Appendix Two.

I mentioned interest rates earlier. They work like this. There exists a thing called the Base Rate, sometimes called the Minimum Lending Rate. This goes up and down according to the state of the economy, or the government's budget requirements. The norm is interest of 5 per cent over Base for business start-up loans, so if the Bank Rate is 10 per cent, you will be paying 15 per cent; if the Bank Rate is 14 per cent, you will be paying 19 per cent. This does not mean that you will be paying the same rate of interest for the whole period of the loan, set when you take it out, but that as the Bank Rate fluctuates, so does your rate of interest.

However, you will almost certainly be repaying some of the principal as you go, so the amount of interest will become less as time goes by. Interest is calculated daily, on the amount of the principal outstanding, so if you should find yourself with some money to spare at any time, it might be worth considering making an extra payment against the principal.

More on raising capital in Chapter Eleven.

3 Finding premises

When you need premises for your business and are wondering where to start looking, there is one basic consideration that supersedes all others. Do your customers come to you, or do you go to them? If you go to them (and I include mail order retailing in this category) your location is not so important, so long as you have an address that is credible. If your customers come to you, however, the precise location of your business is crucial. There are only two sorts of these customers – the ones who set out to come to you, rather than anyone else, and the ones who are known as 'passing trade'.

The passing trade buy from you because you are a handy source of what they want (e.g. sweets, cigarettes, newspapers, a drink or a meal) or because something in your window catches their eye. If you are in the sort of business where you rely on passers-by, you must site yourself in such a position that you can and will be seen by everyone who comes along, and also in a position where they will not pass but pause and come in. You also need to be in a position where plenty of people pass, and will continue to do so for the foreseeable future.

It is no good locating yourself on a busy main road in a position where there are no pedestrians, unless there is obvious and easy parking and motorists can see you in plenty of time to stop. For this reason it is a good idea to get in your car and make a series of approaches to possible sites from both directions and at varied speeds. The hazards to look for are pedestrian crossings, traffic lights, uncrossable central reservations or barriers, one-way systems and anything in the way of parking restrictions which will make the motorist decide to press on to a more accessible place. Advantages are service roads between you and the main road, preferably with parking bays, which have entrances and exits not too far from you, or sets of traffic lights in a position that allows stopped motorists to see you and see how they can get to you and back on to the main road without disrupting their journey too much.

Where pedestrians are concerned, take the trouble to observe the site at different times of day and different days of the week and see what the flow is. Notice the location of bus stops, car parks, cinemas, pubs, supermarkets and the station if there is one (and see when commuters come and go – think of how many of them will buy a newspaper or cigarettes for the train) and make sure the flow is either the same on both sides of the street or heavier on yours. Check also that there are no plans to alter the area radically that will affect that flow. If you depend on those commuters and the station is closed, you may also have to close.

If you are planning a business where the customers come to you deliberately, it is not so necessary to be in a prime location as long as you are findable (advertise!) and there is adequate parking nearby. However, it must be in an appropriate part of town or people will be put off. For instance, mothers would be unlikely to let their young daughters go to dance classes in the sleezy part of town, nor will young upwardly mobile professionals fancy a squash club on an industrial estate.

It is always easier to set up business in an area where you know the local conditions and where you are known yourself. It will often be the local grapevine that tells you a place is for sale before it is advertised, and as often as not it is the availability of such a place that propels the ambition to have your own business from the back to the forefront of your mind. 'I could do a good job of running that', you think. You will need to go and have a good look at it and perhaps ask some questions of the locals which will help you in your decision. Is there going to be a problem in overcoming it's previous poor local reputation, for example? How long will that take? It will not be profitable until the resistance is overcome.

The most common motive for hanging out the For Sale sign is that business is bad, so the first and most important question is – Why is this place available? The next should be – How many people have had it in the last ten years? If the answer to the second question is more than two, you have the answer to the first at hand. For some reason, it is not profitable, and you would be wise to forget it. Are you really that special, that you can make a go of a business where others have failed?

What is the local competition? It is going to be difficult enough getting your new business going without all the aggravation that can come from an unfriendly competitor. It is not unknown in such circumstances for an established shop to sell its goods at a loss for long enough to squeeze out the newcomer. Even if they don't do this, there may not be enough trade to support more than one, so all that happens is that neither of you makes a living.

Before you go any further, you must check the situation on planning permission. Just because the business is currently doing what you want to, it doesn't mean it has permission to do so and you may be forced to close down or revert to the proper use, which could be something you have no interest in, such as an engineering workshop when you want a squash club. If it is not currently what you want you must find out if you can get permission for change of use. It is also wise to write a courtesy letter to the local Chamber of Trade or Commerce. They take a keen interest in the type of trade in their area and also in what they call 'undue competition', and they may lodge objections to your applications for planning permission.

Once you are happy about these aspects, you can ask the last question, which is perhaps the most crucial, and it is not finding the answer to it that has caused the bankruptcy of many inexperienced business people. How much is it going to cost me to run? If you are borrowing money, you must take the interest into account. If the building is in need of redecoration or major alterations, you must take the cost of these into account. And finally you must check on the overheads, rates, insurance etc. Rates are a particularly crucial point. They may be very high and that will do nasty things to your profit margin if you have to compete with someone over the borough border whose rates are lower.

Whichever way you find suitable premises, you must be prepared to pay a lump sum down in addition to the lease/rent. This is called either 'key money' if the place is vacant, or 'a premium' if it is still trading. It is based on a multiple of the weekly takings figure. Anything between thirty and forty-five weeks is normal.

Now for the situations where you go to your customers. If you are manufacturing on any scale, your first enquiry should be to the Industrial Development Officer at the Town Hall, who will know what is available on local industrial estates or if there are any cooperatives with vacancies. These tend to consist of big old buildings converted into one-room workshops and have very reasonable rents, but they are not likely to be suitable for food manufacture.

If you can't find premises this way, try business transfer agents, estate agents, local papers and *Daltons Weekly*. You may be able to sublet from another business with spare capacity, but do check that their lease allows them to do this, or you could find yourself suddenly evicted and unable to claim back any advance rent. If all you want is somewhere to store your goods, you could do worse than a lock-up garage. This will be very cheap, but you will be rather restricted in the type of goods you can store there – nothing that will be damaged by damp air, insects or rats.

If it is offices you want, and you can't find them through the advertisement pages, you need to go to a specialist office-letting agent (*Yellow Pages* again). They will offer you leased or rented premises. If you choose to rent, they will charge you key money, several months' rent in advance, and expect you to agree to a minimum rental period. They will arrange for all the services to be connected, and charge you for doing it. They will also be delighted to organise furniture and fittings and office equipment for you. This is hardly surprising as they will receive commission on it all. Better to organise it yourself and negotiate your own deals over prices!

However you acquire your premises, don't sign anything until you have had the lease/rental agreement checked by your solicitor and a surveyor, who should also inspect the premises. You have to pay for this, but it will be well worth it. Quite apart from the fact that the surveyor might find something nasty which the landlord or previous lease-holder hoped you wouldn't notice, he will be aware of the market forces in the area and will be used to negotiating prices.

The first point to check is that the person offering you the premises is entitled to do so. This means the owner, or his properly authorised agent, or that the lease allows the current holder to assign it to someone other than the landlord. You will want to know whether you can do this yourself in the future, and whether you will be able to sublet.

Has the previous occupant vacated the premises properly, or is there is a dispute? Did he leave them in the condition he should have? If not, and they have to be restored, has he paid for the dilapidations or will you get stuck with them?

Who pays for what in the way of repairs? You or the landlord? If you have to pay for external repairs, the rent should be much lower than if you do not. And who pays for which bits of the building insurance? When does cover commence?

Do you have to pay for maintenance of or dilapidations to shared areas? Are there any restrictions to the use of them, like a clause forbidding you to park a van overnight? Will security men lock the gates at certain times preventing you from working late?

Is there a clause specifying the use to which the premises will be put? Will you be allowed to change it? Will anyone else, if you want to pass the lease on? If the lease is close to its expiry date, will the landlord be prepared to renew it? Or will you be able to purchase the freehold if you want to?

These are just a few of the matters that need to be resolved. There are many more, and many landlords who hope you will let them take advantage of you by committing yourself without checking with someone who knows all the angles.

You may think you can avoid all this by working at home. To a certain extent you can, if you own your home outright, but even then there may be a restrictive clause in the deeds. If you rent, or the property is leasehold, the landlord may object and take steps to stop you. If all you are doing at home is receiving telephone messages and mail, no one will be unduly bothered, but once you start to operate a real office, shop, manufactory or workshop in your dwelling or outbuildings you have changed its established use and must have planning permission. You can use land for any purpose for up to twenty-eight days a year, but the definition of land excludes what is called the 'curtilage' of a building, which basically means gardens and courtyards. So if you have a field or wood, you could use that for almost anything (Adventure games? Nudist conventions? Pony rides?) on those twenty-eight days.

Don't think you will get away with operating a major business at home without planning permission. Even if your neighbours don't 'shop' you, Town Hall staff aren't daft and they can (and do) read business advertisements and put two and two together. They will not like you operating a noisy workshop, or a commercial kitchen, or having a constant stream of callers. You will probably find it easy enough to get permission to use one room as an office, but even this may be restricted to certain hours.

What you must do is inform your house insurers immediately, or you may find you have invalidated both fabric and contents cover. You must also talk to your accountant, especially if your dwelling is jointly owned, for there are tax implications to be considered. While you can claim a proportion of the household overheads (insurance, electricity etc.) as business expenses, you may have to pay capital gains tax on that same proportion of any profit made when the house is sold.

There are other considerations about working from home. I mentioned credibility before in connection with addresses and it occurs again in this context. When you start up, one of your main problems is going to be getting people to take you seriously. This problem will be reduced if you are operating from an obvious commercial address rather than something like '28 Cedar Gardens'.

If you are doing something which allows you to tell

your client/customers that you work from home without losing face, all you have to worry about is concentrating on work instead of being distracted by your environment. I remember one successful consultant telling me she still remembers the day she made the three decisions that revolutionised her life – 'Get a cleaner, get a gardener, get a telephone answering machine.' But even the most sympathetic customer will be unimpressed if your telephone calls are made to background yells of 'Mum, where's my football shirt?', so you are going to have to be very firm with members of your family or other co-habitees in the early days.

You can get over the telephone problem with an appropriate message on an answering machine, except that people who think you should be in a proper office will wonder why you don't have a secretary to answer your phone, and soon work it out. The cheapest answer to this is to use an answering service, where your calls are answered by a real human who responds to requests to talk to you in whatever way you specify – 'She's in a meeting/out with a client/in Germany at a trade fair, can I have her call you back?' or 'Mr Bloggs? She said to tell you she'll be there at noon.' Some of these services are very sophisticated, with the operators sitting in front of a computer which detects which number is being called and flashes your company name and desired response on to a screen for the operator to read.

Telephone answering is only the tip of the iceberg compared with what you can get at 'business centres' (see *Yellow Pages*). For very reasonable fees, these organisations will do everything you need in the way of providing office services. They are so organised that you can pretend you have your permanent office at a prestigious address and no one (except those cynics who take note of such addresses) need ever know otherwise. They will receive and pass on your mail as well as telephone calls. They provide full secretarial services. They have all the latest equipment, from document transmission through telexes to word processors. They will rent you a room, or a suite of rooms, for an hour or a day or week, or the same day each week. They will stage-manage a sales presentation or a conference, provide coffee or an elegant lunch if you want to impress clients. They promise full confidentiality and they charge you for no more than the actual services you use and a small membership fee.

For someone just starting up, they have to be the answer to the office and secretary problem.

4 Getting organised – snags, pitfalls and legalities

Whatever type of business you want to start, you need never fear being short of advice. I have already mentioned the Small Firms Services, which will give you a series of booklets, free information on the telephone and arrange counselling sessions for you. The first three of these sessions are free, then there is a small charge if you need any more. There are also Enterprise Agencies all over the country, which provide advice, counselling and training, often from large firms which are prepared to make their expertise available to small firms or beginners. Contact them through Business in the Community or ask for the booklet on them from the accountants Deloittes, Haskins and Sells.

Most of the Industrial Training Boards have advice services, booklets and newsletters, and of course the trade magazines and newspapers of your chosen field will be full of articles and advertisements from helpful organisations. Ask your library for the appropriate directory listing all of these. Try them all to see what they offer, but with the exception of the government and local government backed organisations, be sure they have no vested interest in the shape of the advice they offer. Just because an organisation has a bland title like 'the Widgetmakers' Association' it does not mean it is not a front for a profit-making, commercial company.

One early decision you must make is the form your own organisation is to take. If you are on your own, you can either operate as a 'sole trader' or start a limited company. If you are setting up a business with other people, you can do it as a partnership – or again start up a Limited

Company. If you have any sense you will do the latter.

I would not advise *anyone* to go into partnership. The risks are too great, even if the other parties do not mean you any mischief. You may all set out with the best of intentions and the same aims, but people do change as time progresses and any of you may find your interests growing away from the point where you started. If you are on your own and this happens to you, you can easily change direction. If not, your partners may not like it. Or it may be they who go off at a tangent and you will find they are spending their time (and the firm's resources) on a ploy of their own.

Family or financial pressures could cause them to behave in ways that you have no control over and you may go to work one morning to find that all the money has been spent on your partner's lover, gambling, addiction or other hobby. There is also a nasty little piece of thinking that allows partners to sell stock or assets and pocket the proceeds on the basis that 'it's half mine anyway'. Maybe it is, but it is also half yours and you will have great difficulty in getting your share from them.

I've heard so many horror stories about partnerships it isn't true. Here is a typical one, which happened to a friend of mine, whom we'll call Henry Higgins. Henry was no business man, but despite my loud protestations he went into partnership with what he thought was another friend, whom we'll call Fred Bloggs. Fred had another shop of his own, where he spent most of his time, while Henry ran the new shop. There was a young female assistant, who was meant to spend her time equally in both shops, but actually spent most of it in Fred's.

Henry was a little indignant when he found the letterheads stated 'The Fred Bloggs Partnership', but he soon accepted it, as he did the suggestion that he should leave all the paperwork to Fred, who was much more experienced.

Henry rather felt that paperwork was beneath him, anyway. After a while, the assistant left, and then Henry found that Fred had accidentally been overpaying her. There was nothing they could do about it, of course, as she had left the area.

It wasn't long afterwards that poor Henry realised he couldn't afford to carry on. His shop wasn't making any money (I told him the location was wrong, but he *would* have that one – Fred liked it) and his bank manager was getting twitchy about the second mortgage. So Henry gave it up, got a job, and left Fred to get rid of the lease. That took a year and it was nearly two more, after a series of rude letters from a solicitor, before Fred produced a set of accounts, and what he said was Henry's share of the money – a miserable £1000. In the meantime, Henry had had to sell his house to pay off the two mortgages and his overdraft. And Fred? He got divorced and married again – to that 'overpaid' assistant!

I thought Henry was lucky to come out of it with any money at all, for Fred liked the ladies, and liked to lavish money on them and his other expensive hobbies. If you are a sole trader and your business fails, your creditors can make you bankrupt and that means that you can lose everything you own, apart from your clothes and the tools of your trade. If you are a member of a partnership, you may also be liable for the debts of your partners (any and all of their debts, not just those relating to the business you are involved in!). You do not even have to sign any formal agreement to be considered a partnership – the definition the courts will apply, if it comes to the crunch, is 'trading in common with a view to profit'.

If your business is run by a limited company, however, that company has a separate legal entity of its own and if that entity goes bankrupt, the property of its owners cannot be seized to pay off its debts. You may lose everything the company owns, but you do not lose your house, your car, or the contents of your personal bank account. It is for that reason that many small businesses are content to put up with the expense and inconvenience of running a limited company. However, it is worth bearing in mind that bank managers may be cagey about lending large sums of money to limited companies which have just been started and in this case may well require you to personally guarantee the loan.

One final thought on bankruptcy. A creditor can start bankruptcy proceedings against you if you owe him as little as £750 and fail to pay. And what is not generally known is that at least half of the country's bankruptcies are brought by either the Inland Revenue against defaulting tax payers, the Customs and Excise against defaulting VAT payers, or the DHSS against people who do not pay for insurance stamps. This last is very easy for the small business to forget, but they always catch up with you in the end!

It does not cost more to set up a limited company than to set up trading on your own account or as a partnership: stamp duties must be paid, certain statutory books must be purchased and so must a company seal. But if you ask a solicitor to set up a company for you, be careful he does not do just that, from scratch. He will spend many costly hours drafting the Memorandum and Articles, and doing all the other bits and pieces, and it will cost you about ten times what it need (don't forget solicitors are in practice to making a living too!).

A better, and quite standard procedure, is for your accountant to purchase a ready-made company, complete with everything needed, from a firm which specialises in starting companies. This is quite cheap as long as you are prepared to accept a neutral name, but if you want a specific name it will cost a little more. There are some restrictions on exactly what you may have as a name for a company (you may not, for instance, use the word 'royal') which do not apply to sole traders or partnerships.

Your accountant will then charge you for preparing the list of shareholders and directors which must be sent to the Registrar of Companies. Next, a limited company has to submit a list of shareholders, directors and other details (called an Annual Return) complete with a copy of the audited accounts, to the Registrar of Companies every year. You must pay a fee every year for the privilege of having these documents filed at Companies House, where anybody can go along and look at them to see what you're doing. Sole traders' and partnerships' accounts do not have to be filed anywhere, and you may prefer to maintain your privacy.

Limited companies are subject to corporation tax on their profits before dividends are paid – which effectively means that you will be taxed twice, as you will also have to pay income tax on the dividends when you receive them. This last point may be purely academic, as you will probably be drawing all the profit as director's salary or putting it into your pension fund. More on that later. There are also certain legal restrictions on exactly what you may and may not do with a limited company and its money, which do not arise with a sole trader or partnership. These may seem good arguments against having a limited company, but they are all offset by the great advantage of having limited liability.

One final point on running your business as a limited company which needs careful consideration is whether you personally want to be employed or self-employed. If you are a sole trader you will be self-employed and get all the tax advantages attached to that status. But you will get very little in the way of social security and unemployment benefits and for this reason you may prefer to be employed, which is easier to organise with a company. There are also some major advantages attached to your pension arrangements.

I keep mentioning accountants and solicitors and other professional advisers. You may be wondering how to find them. The various bodies which run these professions would like you to believe that as long as you choose one of their members all will be well, but alas that is not true. What you have to do for this membership is to study for a few years and pass some exams (many of them in subjects so obscure and pointless that I am convinced their only purpose is to pad out the regulation sixteen exams which these bodies see as a necessity to protect their chartered status), pay a fat annual subscription and keep your nose clean. You do not have to display any commercial acumen nor any commercial competence, nor even practise in all the branches of your chosen profession. For instance, many solicitors spend their entire working life doing nothing but conveyancing and wills.

Innocents tend to assume that professional status conveys a god-like quality on those who have it. Most professionals are perfectly competent, but there are just as many mediocre or disorganised people in the professions as in any other walk of life. Don't risk wasting your time and patience and money and opportunities by picking the first one in the phone book that catches your eye. Ask around until you find an acquaintance whose judgement you trust to recommend one to you, then make sure that the expert is experienced in the particular area that you need help with. And don't forget that they all base their charges on an hourly rate, so don't spend their time if you could do the leg-work yourself. Don't panic, don't witter, don't chat about the weather. You may think you are being friendly, but it is going to be an expensive friendship.

If you are lucky and you run your business sensibly, you may never need to use a solicitor for anything other than property matters. What you will need, on a regular and on-going basis, is a good accountant. No one, unless experienced in the work themselves, should be rash enough to try to operate a business without one. Not only do they know all about taxes, and provide an experienced buffer between you and the Inland Revenue, they will also perform a multitude of other services. They will do your book-keeping, work out salaries and PAYE, do your VAT returns – almost anything you can think of.

As a general guide, it is a good idea to choose an affluent accountant. If he can't handle his own financial affairs properly, he won't do much for yours, either. The one you want is going to suggest to you how you can save tax, without waiting until you ask him how to do it, as well as doing straightforward accounting work. The only proviso is that if you are running a limited company, your accounts must be audited by a chartered accountant.

If you prefer to deal with another woman, you should not have too much difficulty in finding one. Join your local Soroptomists, or plug yourself into one of the women's networks, and you will soon have a source of astute women in all the professions and a number of other occupations which may be useful to you. And you to them – this is a mutual gain situation.

One area where you may not find it so easy to deal with a woman is at your bank, for there are as yet few female bank managers. Given any choice in the matter, I have heard it suggested that an older man is more likely to support you in unusual ventures, as he is more secure in his career progression.

Don't make the mistake of assuming that the average bank manager knows all about business. They do not – they are trained in banking law and banking practice, and unless they have a personal penchant for the other areas of finance which leads them to expertise, all they know about them is what they pick up as they go along. They do not know, in any real depth, about running a business, or insurance, or investments (and yet financial journalists *still* tell people to talk to their bank manager about investment!).

Unless you can find a bank manager who is an expert in your field, you use him for two things only – to borrow from, and to aid you in your day-to-day manipulation of money. That said, you do need to build a good relationship with him and you do this by keeping your nose clean and keeping him in the picture. Tell him what you intend to do and why. Give him as much detail as you can in a form which is readily assimilable. Keep the cash forecasts flowing in his direction. Listen if he warns you of a local trend which may work against you – and give him some feedback for his grapevine. Don't think you can twist him round your little finger and get away with murder. Maybe you can, but Murphy's Law says he'll be on holiday when you do something outrageous, and his stand-in will be one of the auditors from area office.

Bank managers do get moved around at regular intervals. If yours is really good, there is nothing to stop you moving all your accounts to his new branch. Then you continue to pay in and collect cash from the local branch, but the useful decisions are still with your favourite. If you don't want to do this, pay a visit to the new man as soon as you can, to introduce yourself and feel out the new climate. Ask innocently where the previous manager went and if it was to a bigger or smaller or similar branch. If it was an obvious promotion you needn't worry, but if it was a demotion or sideways shuffle, you can be sure the area office weren't too keen on his policies and have put in a new broom.

Either way, this could be your chance to renegotiate your charges. Local managers have some discretion in this, and the threat of moving your accounts could save you half a percentage on your loans or result in a lower charge per entry on your statements. If you do threaten to move, don't dilute your clout by shifting only one account; make it clear that you will take all your accounts, and your husband's and all your staff's. No new incumbent in any job wants his first months marked by a mass exodus of customers.

Incidentally, you must have a separate bank account for the business, even if you are running it as a sole trader. Although your accountant could cope with your doing everything from your own personal account, it means more work for him and therefore more cost for you, as above. And the Inland Revenue won't be keen on it and nor will any prospective purchasers if you want to sell the business.

It is also a good idea to have an overdraft facility. This means that if you need to overdraw, you can do so up to an agreed level – not that you should have a permanently overdrawn balance. The trick with an overdraft is to keep it as low as you can by careful timing on paying your bills, for although the rate of interest will be a couple of points higher than for a formal loan, you only pay it on the amount outstanding on a day-to-day basis. If you are really good at this, you may be able to take advantage of bulk discounts when you are purchasing stock or equipment and still come out on top.

What I am trying to point out here is not merely the advantages of being able to use the bank's money as well as your own, but the necessity, in these inflationary times, for you to develop a financial awareness and look considerably further than the end of your nose.

You must also look to your legal obligations. Many of these are dependent on the type of business, but there are a few that are common to all. Firstly, you must inform the Inland Revenue and the DHSS when you start trading. You must buy National Insurance stamps for yourself on a weekly basis, or arrange to pay monthly by standing order. You must also, in the due course of time (not for at least a year), produce a set of accounts for the Revenue.

You will probably have to register for VAT. The rule is that if your turnover is above a certain level you must register; the level changes each year with the Budget. Note that 'turnover' means takings, not profit, but it does have the proviso that the takings relate to what are called 'taxable' items. Some items are 'exempt' from VAT, others are considered taxable but the tax rate is currently set at zero, and the rest are taxed at standard rate. If in doubt, ask your accountant or your local VAT office. The latter are very helpful, especially when you are starting up. It's only when you are late with your returns, or they think you might be on the fiddle, that they get nasty. And they can get very nasty indeed, for they have powers of search and seizure of anything they think might be relevant. That means your home as well as your business premises.

Once registered you must keep proper records, collect VAT from your customers and hand it on to the Commissioners for Customs and Excise. On registration, you will be given your own VAT number and any invoices you issue must show that number and generally comply with the regulations. You have to submit a quarterly return, showing how much VAT you collected, how much you paid out on purchases, and send a cheque for the difference. When you first start trading, you may well pay out more on equipment and stock than you collect in sales and in this case they will

reimburse you. The forms are quite simple to fill in, but if
you don't want to deal with it yourself, your accountant
will do it for you.

Many of the other obligations relate to the place of work
(particularly if you employ any staff). I have already mentioned planning permission, but you must also pay rates,
comply with fire regulations, and not pollute the environment with noxious substances or noise. You must comply
with the Sale of Goods Act, the Trade Descriptions Act, the
Prices Act, the Weights and Measures Act, the Food and
Drugs Act, the Shops Act . . . This is not meant to be a legal
textbook, but you will have got the idea by now. Ask your
solicitor which of these will affect you and go to the library.

The basic requirement of much of this legislation which
might affect you is that you may need a licence to operate
your business. Some are compulsory – for instance, selling
intoxicating liquors, running an employment agency or
keeping a boarding kennels – and some are at the discretion
of the local authority. Ask the Trading Standards Officer
what you need.

You will be pleased to know that the one area where there
is little compulsion is insurance policies. You must have
'employers' liability' cover if you have staff, and you must
have 'Road Traffic Act' cover as a minimum if you operate
vehicles on the road. Anything beyond that is up to you, but
unless you have a special arrangement with God, you had
better do the sensible thing and call on a good insurance
broker, or your tame 'tied' agent, who will have all the
necessary contacts.

Where vehicles are concerned, you really should have
'fully comprehensive' cover on your vehicles. Driving
around in a damaged vehicle does nothing for your image
and you may not be able to afford to have it repaired
without insurance. Nor may you be able to afford to replace

stock that was stolen from it or with it. Just be sure to tell the insurance company you are using the vehicle for your business, or they may decline to pay out. The stock itself will need 'stock in transit' cover.

If you are running a shop, you can cover all the other items you need by taking out a special 'shopkeepers' package. This will include all the possible events that could happen to the building or customers or staff, from fire and flood to riots or bits dropping off aeroplanes, as well as theft of stock, equipment or cash, broken windows, employers' liability and public liability.

This last one covers members of the public while they are actually on your premises and for objects which might injure them when they are passing, such as bits falling off your building or bits sticking out. It also covers you for the situation where an item you recommended to a customer has proved faulty and caused an accident. (Some insurance companies class this separately as 'product liability'.) Considering the size of some recent awards for injuries leading to incapacity, you would be well advised to ensure that you are adequately covered. Cover of £2 million is not excessive.

Incidentally, you should keep an accident book and enter all accidents, however trivial. Even a small cut on a finger could lead to blood poisoning if neglected. You could have forgotten all about it months before a claim is made. If you can prove from your accident book that you applied appropriate first aid, you will save yourself a good deal of hassle. Just list the date and time, name of the victim, cause of the injury, nature of the injury and the action taken. In the event of a death or 'major' injury (one which puts the victim into hospital for twenty-four hours) you must also report it to the Environmental Health Department. If you are unfortunate enough to have a death on your premises, you must immediately report it to the police.

If you do not have a shop, you will have to deal with each type of insurance separately. Do not forget to cover your office equipment and manufacturing machinery, and consider whether you also need 'consequential loss' cover. This only comes into play when disaster strikes your premises and prevents you trading. It may not give you all your lost potential profit, but it will provide for fixed expenses such as rent, wages etc., which have to be paid even if you are not trading.

The other insurances you should consider are the ones which concern you personally. The most important of these is on your life. Don't think you don't need it – unless you are a childless unmarried orphan, you do. It's not as if it were expensive – basic, no frills, pay-out-only-if-you-die, 'term' life assurance is the cheapest thing in the world,* and you can still get tax relief on it.

You should also give some thought to health insurance. There are 'sickness and accident' policies which pay you a monthly sum if you are ill or injured and thus cannot work, and 'permanent health' policies which will pay you until retiring age if you are permanently incapacitated. There are also private medical schemes, such as BUPA, which pay for you to have private treatment at a time convenient to you. Not only do they cover you for the ills that can strike anyone, they also cover you for gynaecological treatment (except childbirth). Even the common 'women's' ailments can drag you down dreadfully, and the menopause comes to all of us. Imagine trying to run your business feeling increasingly ill for the two or more years it can take to get treatment on the National Health.

Those are items you can deal with straightaway. What

* For a thirty-year-old woman, covering her life for £100,000, until she is fifty, costs less than £15 a month.

you should also consider, but cannot take action on until you have been trading for a year (because the amount of your contribution is based on your accounts for that year) is a pension plan. Don't make the classic mistake of assuming that you will be able to sell your business when you retire and live off the proceeds. You might, but that presupposes that someone will want to buy it. What if your lease is about to expire, or there is to be a motorway built through your premises? What if nobody wants your buggy-whips or linoleum any more? And anyway, will it be worth enough to keep you in luxury for the rest of your days if inflation is still with us? Far more sense to make proper provision for your retirement, especially if you can do it instead of paying lots of tax.

Pension plans for both the self-employed and company directors are marketed (and their investments managed) by life assurance companies. They are tremendously tax advantageous to the extent that you may be able virtually to eliminate any tax liability perfectly legally. As you might suppose, with such advantages, these schemes are extremely complex and you will need to consult both your accountant and a financial expert who is experienced with these plans. Most ordinary insurance brokers are not.

There is another advantage of paying into a pension plan, which is that you can use it to raise a loan. The security is the lump sum at retirement and you can borrow up to fifteen times your annual contribution. These loans can be cheaper than other types, but once again you need to consult an experienced expert.

5 Accountancy

One of the most enlightening pieces of reading matter to come my way recently was a statistical report on the reasons for small business failure, produced by the Official Receiver's office. The most telling thing about it was the different reasons given in each case, by the proprietors of the businesses and the Official Receiver.

The proprietors blamed things which they obviously felt were beyond their control – poor staff, too much competition, difficult customers, bad debts, bad weather and so on. They all thought they had been unlucky, which to my mind is a dreadful cop-out. All those reasons listed are avoidable or curable, given a little forethought, observation and proper control – but it's so much easier to let things drift and say 'It wasn't my fault, I was unlucky.' I don't remember who it was who first said it, but on being congratulated on his luck in being successful, he replied 'Funny thing, the harder I work, the luckier I get!'

In business, you get lucky by constant attention to detail, and you stay out of trouble by keeping a close watch on the financial details. Which reflects what the Official Receiver had to say about those failures. He blamed 67 per cent of them on managerial incompetence – specifically lack of control over assets and liabilities, costs, sales, and what he termed 'granting excess credit'. In other words, failing to ensure that bills were paid on time (or at all).

I have heard it suggested that you should pay all your bills and send out all your invoices on the same day each month. I don't agree, and my reasons are based on inflation and the cost of credit, and VAT. I have already suggested that you should delay paying your bills for the sake of your overdraft, and for the same reason you should encourage your customers to pay theirs as soon as possible by sending invoices promptly. Even without an overdraft you want the money in your hands, where you can make it work for you. Don't leave it to languish in a current account either – put it somewhere to earn some interest.

The point about VAT on purchases is that although it is reclaimable it is not, as some people think, free. You do not get it back until you do your quarterly returns, so if you pay for equipment or stock at the beginning of the quarter you have lost the use of the VAT element until the end of the quarter. VAT on sales is due on the date of the invoice, not when you get paid, so if you have a batch of invoices to send out near the end of the quarter, you should ideally delay until the returns have been done. That way, you don't have to pay the VAT man money you haven't collected.

Other than when you want to indulge in such judicious juggling, you should get invoices out fast, and reminders out even faster, if you don't get paid in the stipulated time. It is generally accepted that thirty days' credit is the norm, but it does no harm to state it on your estimates, printed terms of business, contracts, and any letters you may write to potential customers at the negotiating stage. If you are operating in any sort of a sellers' market (one where you condescend to deal with people on your terms, not go begging for their business on theirs) you can even state in your terms of business that you add interest to bills not paid within a certain time. If they are really anxious to have your goods or services, you could even demand a down payment before you start, or term payments at regular intervals during the job. This last is common practice in the building trade, for instance, and by no means unknown with consultants.

Incidentally, don't give credit to anybody until you've checked them out. It's a reasonable assumption that ICI are not going to go bust (mind you, we all thought that about Rolls Royce, didn't we?) or leave the country without paying you, but you shouldn't trust anybody less. Don't be fooled by flashy offices or big cars or all the other trappings of affluence. They can all be obtained on credit, and most of them are. So check.

Ask new customers for two trade references and where they bank. With the trade referees you write a letter on the lines of 'Bloggins and Co. have given us your name for a business reference. Would you please confirm that their dealings with you have been above board and that you have not had any difficulties with their account.' Don't forget to enclose a reply-paid envelope.

The bank reference you take up through your bank, asking them to check if Bloggins are honourable and good for the amount they want on credit. Rather like estate agents' language, the reply needs a little interpreting, but if it says 'certain/undoubted/good for your figure' you have no need to worry; if it says 'should be good' it means there is a little risk; 'considered respectable, would not enter into commitments he couldn't fulfil' means he doesn't usually have that sort of money, or they're not sure of him; and 'unable to speak for your figure/purpose' means they don't want to commit libel but you should stay clear.

There are also commercial enquiry agents who will do all this for you and take up a reference with one of the trade associations. They will dig very deeply if you want. Obviously they cost quite a bit, but it could save you making a dreadful mistake. Many of them also handle debt collecting.

If it does come to the point where your second invoices, statements, 'you may have overlooked this' stickers and telephone calls have all failed to produce a payment, you may consider handing the problem over to professional debt collectors. They are not likely to be interested in small amounts, unless you have a lot of them, and they will want a fee or a percentage of what they recover. Either way, it will probably be cheaper than getting your solicitor to sue.

Many small debtors are frightened into paying by a letter from a solicitor threatening legal action, and this does not cost very much. The costs start to mount up when a writ is issued, but this frightens another set of people into paying – the ones who realise you are not bluffing and don't want a stain on their credit record. Others do not react, or file a defence and you then have to decide whether the cost of going on is worth the risk of losing your case and having to pay both lots of cost. Even if you do win, if the amount is small (£500 or less) you will get no costs, and if it is a County Court, the judge may listen to the defendant's pleas of poverty and order him to pay £5 a month for as long as it takes.

This is one of the reasons why professional debt collectors ignore the County Courts. These courts also take a *very* long time to do anything, and may agree to transfer the case to the debtor's home town, which delays everything again. The professionals use the High Court, where the judge gives a judgement only, and leaves you to collect the money how you like – sheriff, bailiffs, or bankruptcy proceedings – and where if there is no defence filed within fourteen days of the writ being served, you can apply for, and get, 'judgement in default of a defence'.

If you want to try the County Court route, you can do it without a solicitor. Ask the Registrar's department for the booklet on 'Small Claims' (under £500). You will find his staff very helpful, but they are not allowed to give legal advice, so word your questions carefully.

There is one way you can avoid all this trouble and that is to hand your sales ledger over to factors. They will only handle a large ledger (where the annual turnover is in excess of £250,000) and it is really only a one-off benefit. They pay you up to 80 per cent of the total invoice value immediately and the rest, less their fee, when they have collected it. However, check with your capital lender first. Debtors are considered to be an asset and if your lender has a floating charge over all your assets they won't like you factoring your debts.

In a retail business, none of this need be a problem. Now that credit cards and bank guarantee cards are so common, there is no reason why you should allow *anybody* to run a credit account. You should not accept cheques without the guarantee card, and then you do not need to go through the stupid routine of asking the customer to put their address on the back of the cheque. Many people are so incensed by this that they put a made-up address on principle, or refuse to buy from you. A bank guarantee card only guarantees cheques of *up to* £50 and not, as some people think, £50 worth of larger cheques, so you must keep to this top limit. You must see the cheque being signed (a second time on the back if necessary) and must check the signature with the card. The code number must be written on the back of the cheque by you or your staff, not the customer, and it does no harm to add the card's expiry date as well.

If someone wants to give you a cheque for substantially more, tell him he can collect the goods in a week and consult your bank. They will check with his and find out if he has the sum involved, in which case you pay the cheque in on 'special clearance'. Ask how much the bank will be charging you for this and the enquiry, then you can decide whether to make the customer pay it.

The other things to watch out for with cheques are people you don't know who suggest you should give them cash for a cheque, or people who try to hurry you into accepting a cheque, or who appear to be mortally offended if you ask for identification, and youngsters who may be under age and therefore not legally responsible for their debts.

The safest way to accept payment for goods is by credit card. There is no point in anyone's stealing the completed vouchers, as they are imprinted with your shop's name and code number and are therefore of no value to anyone else. They cannot be endorsed to a third party, as stolen cheques can, and providing you have kept to the rules laid down by the credit card company you are guaranteed payment even if it turns out that the card was stolen or the card-holder was over his credit limit. They also mean less cash on your premises to tempt sticky fingers.

The rules are simple. When you sign your agreement with the company, they will give you what they call a 'floor limit'. You must not process payments over this limit without telephoning for authorisation, when you will be given an authorisation number to put on the slip.

Another advantage of cards over cheques is that you do not have to wait for clearance before you can be sure the money is in your bank. You pay the vouchers into your bank and the money is credited to your account immediately – all of it as shown on the vouchers. All it costs you is a small joining fee and a monthly service charge. This varies according to the volume of business you do, but is normally a little over 2 per cent. If you want to accept postal or telephone credit card business, you have to have an additional agreement.

The security aspect is a major advantage with credit cards, but there is another just as important. Customers are more likely to buy expensive items from you if they can pay by credit card, so it could give you the edge on a competitor who doesn't accept them.

Whether it is credit cards, cheques or cash you are taking, you should go to the bank every day, as it is easier for all the parties concerned in your accounts if your bankings correspond with your till rolls. If anyone other than you personally uses the till, it is also a good idea to empty it of all but its float at some point during the day, or more than once if you are taking a lot of money. Take a sub-total from the till and make sure the cash and cheques etc. correspond. This is the best way of checking if you have light-fingered helpers and the best deterrent against this problem.

Most tills produce a roll of paper with the day's transactions printed on them and you should keep these as part of your accounting records. Hopefully the Inland Revenue will never want to see them, but your accountant will and the VAT man might.

If you are selling a mixture of items that do or do not bear VAT, you will need some method of keeping them separate in your takings record. Find some method of showing which is which on the actual goods – coloured price tags is the easiest, then all you need is the same colours on the till 'department' buttons. Most tills have these buttons and will produce a set of sub-totals for each at the end of the day. Older tills usually have ten buttons, new electronic machines many more. With this division already done for you by the till, it is then very easy to transfer the figures to your books.

Whatever business you are in, you must keep an accurate record of all the money you take and all the money you spend. Remember that VAT inspectors may call and demand to see your records. Woe betide you if they are not up to date. You may also find, if you cannot produce accurate records, that your tax inspector will make an 'estimated assessment' (jargon for a semi-blind guess) of your profits and demand tax accordingly. It is then up to you to appeal for an interview with the Commissioners and prove the assessment is wrong. You do not have much time to do this.

Quite apart from these reasons, you should keep proper records for your own sake, for without them you cannot get any idea of how you are doing, nor can you plan properly for the future. Unless you are issuing a lot of invoices to a lot of separate customers, you do not even have to get involved in the complexities of 'double entry' book-keeping. (Even this can be simplified by investing in one of the kits sold by any business stationer.)

The simplest form of book-keeping is where you just list everything, without attempting to analyse it. Get a ruled book from the stationers, use the left-hand page of each pair for income and the right-hand page for outgoings. This is the conventional way of doing it, so don't confuse your accountant's staff by being different. Make a note each day of how much you have paid into the bank and how much you have paid out. Keep all invoices and receipts. This will take you about thirty minutes a week and it is the minimum you must do. It is going to take your accountant a long time to unravel it all and check it against your bank statements and he will charge you accordingly. It is a method that does not give you much information to help you with your planning, either.

The other way to keep books is only a little more time-consuming for you, but saves your accountant hours of tedious work. It also provides you with at-a-glance information on your financial affairs. For this, you'll need a little more in the way of books. You'll need one book for petty cash and one for bank transactions. Both will need to be ruled in cash columns, with a wide column on the left for details and dates. The petty cash book needn't be large, as it will need only about six columns per page, but the cash book will need several columns for income and about ten for expenditure. You can buy these books ready ruled at any business stationers. It does no harm to have two sets, which you use in alternate years, while your accountant deals with the other set at his leisure.

For the cash book, starting a new page for each month, head up the columns for the items you receive regularly and spend on regularly, allowing one column for the VAT element in each case. Keep the first column on each side for basic bank details. The entries on the expenditure side should consist of cheques paid out, any standing orders you might have, and charges made by the bank. The entries on the income side should correspond with your paying-in book.

When you write a cheque, fill in the stub with not only the date and amount of money, but the name of the person you paid and the item you paid for – and if VAT was involved, the amount of that. (Example – 12 June. Bloggs & Co., wholesale. Invoice No. 1489. VAT £150, goods £1000, total £1150.) Then all you have to do at cash book time is put down the name, date and cheque number, the amount of the cheque in the first column and allocate the amounts as above in the appropriate columns. For both income and expenses, there will be items that crop up occasionally, but not often enough to have a column of their own, like an insurance premium or the three-monthly payment to the VAT man. For this purpose, you have a column marked 'other', with a space next to it where you can note what it was.

For the petty cash book, you do not need so much detail, as the only income will be when you cash a cheque for this purpose. The expenditure will be such items as coffee for the morning break, or stamps from the post office.

You should write up the books every week and then spend another hour at the end of the month adding up all the columns and putting the invoices in order. Put a paper clip on each month's collection and put them away safely. With those columns added, you can not only see how you are doing, but your VAT return will be easier and you will have figures handy for your cash flow forecasting.

'Cash flow forecasting' is a fancy name for budgeting, which is a concept that seems to terrify people. This is a nonsense, for it is easy to do. You know you must pay certain expenses, like the electricity bill, at certain times, and you know you will have other regular expenses, like petrol. You also must have some idea what income you will have and when it will come, so all you have to do is arrange the figures in columns on a monthly basis.

Get two large sheets of ruled and columned paper – you will need a wide column on the left for details and eighteen small ones for figures. On the first sheet, taking two columns per month, head up the first twelve columns for the next six months of the year. The next four columns will be for the last two quarters of the year and the final two for totals. You should now have pairs of columns marked January, February, March, April, May, June, July to September, October to December, Total. Head up the second sheet in quarter years and totals and that gives you the next two years. Finally, mark each pair of columns 'actual' and 'budget'.

Now for the details. Use the top of the page for income and the rest for expenses. Allow three lines at the bottom for totals, balances and cumulative balances. Allow one line for each item you spend on (rent, loan repayment, rates, wages, stock etc.) and make sure you have one marked 'contingencies'. This is for the disasters that can hit you when you least expect them. If you allow some money to deal with them, they won't hurt so much. Don't forget to include your own wages when it comes to expenses.

Having done that, you can begin to put in some figures. Work out how much each item earns/costs each month and fill in the budget columns. Don't forget to multiply by three for the 'quarters' columns and don't forget seasonal variations. This will be easy enough for the first six months, as you can be fairly sure what things cost, but you must make allowances for inflation further ahead. I would suggest a 5 per cent increase every six months.

Having done this – and you must make allowances for *everything* – you can then add up the columns. First total the income and expenses, then deduct expenses from income and put the result in the balance line. If expenses are more than income and you get a minus figure, put brackets round it. This is an accounting convention to indicate a minus figure. Now you can do the cumulative balances. Just add the month's balance to the previous month's cumulative balance. Hopefully this will increase steadily as the months progress, but it may go into negative figures at times.

You now have an advance picture of your business's development or decline. It may scare the living daylights out of you, but it will tell you the truth about your chances of success or bankruptcy. It will prepare you for the lean months, so you have cash ready, instead of that panic to sell something below its real value to pay the bills. It will tell you when you will be able to afford a new word-processor, or if you can afford the repayments on a loan to extend your office. It will also convince your bank manager not only that you can afford those repayments, but that you are a responsible business woman, instead of a feckless fool blundering blindly along in the dark, hoping that everything will turn out all right in the end.

One final point about these cash flow forecasts. The more you do them, the better your guesstimates of amounts will become, and here is where those 'actual' columns come in. Every month, when you add up the columns in your cash books, fill in the actual column on your cash flow forecast. Then you can compare 'actual' with 'budget' and see how accurate your guesstimates were – and prove that accuracy to your bank manager. (An example of a cash flow forecast is shown in Appendix One.)

One other bit of jargon I should mention is 'overtrading', which is often cited as a cause of failure. As with all these terms, the actual concept is quite simple, but that doesn't make it any less of a danger. What it means is that you don't have enough liquid capital to pay all your bills today if you had to. Liquid capital is ready money – the stuff you can lay your hands on easily. Stock and work in progress doesn't count because you cannot turn it into enough immediate cash.

Imagine you are a contract gardener. You have a full order book, all jobs for district councils whom you know will pay without any difficulty when the jobs are completed. That won't be for some months, but today you have to pay the office rent and your assistant and the seed suppliers – and you have already exceeded your overdraft limit. You have plenty of work, but you cannot finance it – that's overtrading.

So is the situation where you have lots of work, but got your sums wrong when you priced the jobs. If it costs you £10 to make a widget and another £7 to pack it and advertise it and you sell it for £16, you will never make a profit, no matter how many you sell. In fact, the more you sell, the worse it gets.

But suppose you sell it for £18? You've made a profit,

haven't you? Great, for every widget you sell, you have £1 all of your very own. Wrong again, I'm afraid. You have made a profit, but it is called gross profit and it is subject to tax. When the taxman has had his bit, what is left is called net profit and that is what you get to keep. So obviously, the less the taxman gets, the more you get and so we come back to the point I keep labouring, which is that a good accountant is worth his weight in gold, for his tax know-how will save you more than his fee.

Taxation is a complex field and since each Budget tends to change the situation, the help of an expert to maximise opportunities is essential. All you have to understand is the difference between tax evasion and tax avoidance. Evasion is illegal and dishonest, as it involves deliberately taking action to evade paying tax that is lawfully due. Avoidance is perfectly legal and it hinges on a famous court decision that said there is no legal bar to arranging one's financial affairs in such a way as to reduce one's tax liability to a minimum.

The main area in which a small business can reduce its tax liability is by ensuring that all legitimate expenses have been claimed. These are the ones that relate to the running of the business. Coffee for the proprietor's home use is not, but coffee for the staff's morning break is and so are the chairs they sit on while they drink it. Petrol for the delivery van is, petrol for your motoring holiday might be if you visit some customers *en route*, petrol for your morning trip to deliver the children to school is not.

What all this boils down to is that you must keep a note of *all* expenditure (and bills, if possible) and let your accountant decide what is legitimately claimable. And if you are considering making any radical changes in your field of operation, buying any expensive equipment or even changing your car, consult him first. It might be advantageous to time these moves according to your year end, the last budget, or just your general situation. Trust your accountant and let him utilise the fiscal skills you are paying for to your best advantage.

Some more thoughts on losses. From an accountant's point of view, a loss is not always the disaster it may appear to the layman. If it goes on too long, the taxman will begin to wonder how you manage to eat regularly and start to probe deeper, but on a short-term basis (like about four years) it may even turn out to be advantageous. The Inland Revenue are a bit suspicious of married women, in case the husband is using his wife's hobby as a tax loss device, but providing you can prove you are running your business with 'a view to profit' they will not object too much. But beware those words and if you get a letter from the Inland Revenue using them, be sure to consult your accountant before answering. Come to think of it, it is a good idea to consult him every time before talking or writing to them. They have a sneaky habit of asking superficially innocent but actually carefully worded questions that need equally carefully worded answers. You can avoid this sort of problem, and maybe even those awful visitations from the VAT man, by having your registered business address at your accountants and keeping your books there.

How can a loss be turned to advantage? When you first start up in business, you can set the losses from your first four years' trading against your income from the preceding three years, which means a rebate. Even when you have been operating for a long time, losses from one year can be set against profits from the next and this reduces the tax on the profitable year. If you are self-employed, you are still entitled to a personal allowance, which means you pay no tax on the first chunk of your income. If that allowance is £2000 and your business shows a profit of £2060 for the year after last year's loss has been deducted, you will only have to pay tax on £60.

Better yet, losses from one business can often be set against earned income from another source, with the same result. So, if you are running a business on the side and have another job, or if you and your husband are taxed jointly, he works and you run a business which makes a loss, that loss can be used to reduce the tax liability from the job. And since the tax on the job will already have been paid by PAYE, the end result is a tax rebate.

6 Getting organised – the practicalities

I've already stated this, but it is worth repeating. People judge you by first impressions. So don't jump the gun by opening for business before you have everything ready, or whatever grapevines apply to your chosen niche will hum with the message, 'Don't bother about her, she hasn't got the faintest idea of what she's doing.'

The sad thing is that if you don't get your act together properly, you will never know how much business you have lost. It is not the British way to complain, we just go away and don't come back. Think of all the small businesses that have irritated you with amateurish fumbling and then count how many of them are still functioning.

No matter what you are doing, nor on how small a scale, the least you owe yourself is to do it professionally. With this in mind, almost the most important job when you are setting up is to get proper letterheads and business cards. Proper means not only a good printing job, it means a design that is appropriate to your market. Working as I do in the world of banking and slick marketing, when I saw a letterhead from a shop broker recently, my first reaction was 'Oh dear, how downmarket and amateurish.' It was on square paper, in plain black, and rather crudely printed. But when I thought about it, I realised he had actually got it right. His clients are mostly back-street shopkeepers in the rough end of town and they would be frightened off by sophistication.

(Mind you, there is one thing to be said for plain black in any situation. It can be easily and cheaply reproduced on a good photocopier. People who design and print stationery will tell you colours add class. But then they would, wouldn't they? It means more work and money for them.)

Don't be tempted to cut corners and do it yourself with those stencil lettering sets either. Unless you are a skilled graphic artist, the end result always looks shoddy. (Beware of cheap print shops, too, for this is how they do it.) Don't forget your letterhead is the first thing most suppliers and non-retail customers see of you, so make sure it tells them what you want it to. For this reason, it is better to put 'Bloggs and Co. (trading as "The Gift Shop")' than 'The Gift Shop (Proprietor B. Bloggs)'. Why? Well, how many 'gift' shops do you suppose there are? How do you expect despatch clerks or anyone else to know which one? Worse than this is to use something terribly twee, or a dreadful pun. It will pall on you soon enough and it will make suppliers and customers cringe.

Another manifestation of this is to have silly messages on your answering machine. I had occasion recently to ring a couple of local word-processing bureaux, and found one of them had a series of clever clever messages on their machine. There were imitations of Peter Sellers and Arthur Daley, a Frankenstein and several others. I laughed at them, but then wondered if they would play the fool with my work, too, and gave it to their competitor.

Answering machines are not a toy, they are a business tool and they are one of your fronts to the big wide world. The best messages are the ones that say 'Bloggs and Company. I'm sorry there is no one here at the moment, but if you leave your number we'll call you back.' The best sort of machines have a remote interrogation device, so you can collect messages by calling from outside.

Forget the adverts for mobile or car telephones. Unless you are in some sort of business where you cannot call home at intervals to collect messages, or it really is a matter of life and death for people to get hold of you urgently (be honest with yourself about this) you do not need one. If people really want to talk to you, they'll ask you to call back or keep trying until they get you. Yes, I know it would be fun to have one, and it would do wonders for your image, but they are horrendously expensive to acquire and to run. There is, however, a lot of commission in them for the sellers and they will do their best to persuade you they are essential.

Let's just pause here for a minute and think about this 'image' business. If your reason for wanting to go into business is that you fancy the idea of dashing about in a fast car, doing deals and generally appearing important, I have to tell you that you can do all that stuff working for someone else. That way, you do it on their money, not yours. You do of course have to be damn good to get a job with perks like that. Well, I'm sorry lady, you also have to be damn good working for yourself, if you want to do enough business to be able to afford all the trappings. Sure, you can get them all on credit as soon as you start up in business, but they will soon melt away if you don't earn enough to keep up the payments. Coming home on the bus from your bankruptcy hearing is not going to enhance your image one little bit.

This is why the first piece of office equipment you should buy is a very large wastepaper bin for all the sales literature that will start arriving as soon as you make any sort of public announcement. You'll need to learn to recognise a sales pitch on the telephone too, and how to cut it off short, or you will spend all your time listening to one spieler after another.

If they come right out and tell you they are selling something, you have the options of saying 'I've got one', 'I'm not even remotely interested', or 'I'm not prepared to talk about it until I've seen your literature and everyone else's – put yours in the post and I'll think about it', followed by,

'Thank you. Goodbye.' If they don't want to admit they are selling something – one of the favourite ploys is 'We're conducting a survey' – you have the options of hanging up without comment, hanging up after a polite or rude version of 'Go away, I'm busy' or placing the receiver on your desk and ignoring it, which keeps the line open and prevents them making any more calls until you replace it. You'll find that discourages even the most persistent ones quite effectively. (Incidentally, if you are planning to do some telephone selling yourself, this should give you some insight into the hazards of this method of approach.)

Most of these nuisances are perpetrated by either 'telesales' staff trying to make appointments for a salesman, or by novice salesmen who have to prove themselves on small businesses before they are allowed to play in the big league. They all get paid commission on sales and they all have quotas to meet. If they exceed the quotas, they get bonuses; if they consistently fail to meet them, they get fired. Either way, they have a big incentive to develop a hard skin.

They will want you to buy office equipment, telephones, exhibition space and various types of advertising. This latter will range from giveaways with your name on (plastic paperclips, pencils, book matches etc.) to actual advertising space in magazines. You can't afford any of it when you first start up, and you can do better deals other ways when you are established, so choke them all off. Beware particularly the latest naughty trick among ad-space salespeople, which occurs when you have placed an advertisement in a magazine or newspaper. 'We've seen your ad in the *Bloggtown Gazette*,' they say, and you think they are a customer. Then, 'We can repeat the same ad in our *Higginshire Journal* series. We can copy this one and that way it won't cost you anything for the artwork. We're doing a special series next month on your trade and we thought you'd like to be in that.'

If you say anything other than 'No!' very firmly (and to be quite safe follow it up with a letter to the advertising manager complaining about his pushy sales staff and stating that you *do not* wish to advertise) you will receive in the post, when it has already been published, a copy of the relevant paper with your advertisement in it, accompanied by an invoice for several hundred pounds. If you don't pay it, they will sue, and win, for the advert was published and it is only your word against theirs on the true events. By this time, of course, the salesperson will have moved on to another job with the commission on your ad long since spent.

There is another hazard with salesmen who want you to buy large capital items, such as machinery, whether it be for the office or the workshop. Since these items usually cost several thousand pounds, the problem of how you might pay for them arises. You may think you have the perfect get-out by stating that you can't afford that sort of money, but they are ready for that. 'I will show you how you can afford it,' they say, and they reach for their finance house leaflets. There are three things you should know about this situation.

The first is that the interest rate on this sort of loan is not far off double what you would pay your bank if you borrowed the money from it. Get out your calculator and do the sums for yourself. Do not believe salesmen who try to tell you that 30 per cent APR over three years is 10 per cent per annum. It isn't – APR means Annualised Percentage Rate.

The second thing is that the salesman earns a fat chunk of commission from the finance deal, which is part of the reason why the rates are so high, as well as his normal commission on the machine. (So, incidentally, do car salesmen, which is why they are not in the least bit interested in cash deals.) This gives you a fair bit of leverage with the salesman, which I'll come back to in a minute.

The third thing is that if you do take a loan for the machine, you are committed to that loan and its repayments whether or not the machine is any use. I don't mean functional breakdowns. These will be covered by a guarantee (you've checked that, haven't you?). What I do mean is that if the machine turns out to be less than what you needed, or something you didn't need at all, you are lumbered with it and with paying for it. There's an old saying that goes 'If you're going to take a long-term car loan, don't buy a short-term car.'

You'll be very lucky to get 50 per cent of the machine's cost back, even if you sell it the week after you bought it, and that won't get the lender off your back. Finance companies are not prepared to mess about with defaulters. They just go into their standard routine of two rude letters, solicitor's letter, writ, judgement and bankruptcy.

If you really do want the machine, you keep this fact from the salesman until you have explored all the angles; find out all you can on the competition and their prices. Give him cups of coffee and indulge in a little social chitchat and see if he will talk about his sales record and the company reward system. What you want to know is whether your purchase is just another deal to him, or whether it will get him into the bonuses or to the annual convention. It is even worth, before you start investigating machines, trying to find out the different companies' cut-off date for convention qualification.

This is where the leverage comes in. If he is anxious to qualify for the convention (they get free trips to all sorts of exotic places) or if he is really hard up and desperate for commission, you should be able to get lots of freebies thrown in with the machine. Floppy discs for word-processors, paper for photocopiers, ribbons for typewriters are all 'disposables' for salesmen who have to demonstrate machines, and it won't hurt him to give you a big stack of them. If he pleads a boss who won't let him do it, make him bring the boss to see you. Bosses have quotas to meet, too, and a lot of kudos to earn from getting their team to the convention. You may even manage to negotiate a cash incentive to sign the order form, but don't sign until you have the goodies safely in your store room.

All of the above presupposes that you actually want to buy the equipment outright, which for tax reasons you usually don't. If you buy capital items you can only claim a percentage of the cost against your year's income, whereas if you rent or lease, the whole of that cost in the year is deductable.

Renting is not easy, but leasing is. Be sure the agreement is for an 'operating' lease, not a 'lease purchase' as the Revenue considers the latter to mean you have bought the machine when you make the first payment. The way it works is that you tell the leasing company *exactly* what you want (a 'Higgins and Wiggins' Mark 624A multiple widget grinder). They do the normal credit referencing on you, buy the machine new from the manufacturers and lease it to you. It remains their property, although the usual routine is that at the end of the leasing period they write and ask if you want to continue the lease, or to buy the equipment. The purchase price quoted is nominal. I am told by those who have done it that if you don't bother to reply, or tell them you don't want the machine any more, they rarely bother to collect it.

But you don't need to buy new at all if you're short of money. There is plenty of good second-hand equipment around, without your having to look very hard for it. There's *Exchange and Mart*, second-hand dealers, auctioneers specialising in bankrupt stock, and the small ads in your trade magazine. If you have a choice, go for the one that has had a service contract (which you'll want to see) but, in any case, make sure it has all its parts with it. If anything is missing be sure you can get replacements and find out how much they will cost to buy and fit.

The one thing that is not wise to buy second-hand, unless you really know what you are doing, is a computer. Mind you, the same thing applies to new ones. There are so many variables in the way of memory size, peripherals and software that you need an expert to guide you if you are not one yourself. If you're not an expert, or at the very least well experienced, you should not be buying a computer at all. Even the most 'user friendly' machines take time to get used to, and you cannot spare that time from the more important task of running your business. And what will you do when something goes wrong? It is more usually a software or operator fault than a mechanical or electronic fault, so you can't just send for a repairman.

What do you want the thing for anyway? Don't let computer buffs kid you that they are the best and fastest way of running an office system. Until you get to the stage of needing to handle more than a thousand invoices, stock items or customers' records a month, you can do it more cheaply (and probably just as fast) with your head, index cards, a calculator and a typewriter.

Don't forget you have to spend time putting information into the machine before it can deal with it, or you have to pay someone else to put that information in. If you do have vast amounts of information to deal with on a regular basis, you will probably still find it cheaper and considerably less hassle to get a service bureau to do the whole thing for you.

As with anything else, shop around and compare prices. Don't forget to consider the cost of another human to do the work manually as an alternative. And finally, ask yourself Macdonald's Question – 'Do I really need it?'

You can apply this to many other items of equipment. Remember that you're in business to make money, not throw it away on expensive equipment. You do need access to a tame typist or a good typewriter of your own – very old ones and portables produce amateurish letters. You do need a reliable calculator of some sort – inaccurate quotations and invoices are also amateurish and beg delayed payments. You probably don't need a photocopier, or not until your volume of essential copying reaches the point where your own machine really would cost less than the local franchise. If money is really tight, you can make a perfectly serviceable filing system out of used brown envelopes and cardboard boxes.

While you should not skimp on the items outsiders see, especially your letter paper and envelopes, you can make do with cheaper versions of most stationery. Ball-points work as well as gold-plated fountain pens, and a chain-store diary is just as useful as a leather-bound one with a load of extraneous information bulking it out. A big day-to-a-page diary, or a plain notebook, makes a perfectly good substitute for those horrendously priced 'personal organiser' systems, and in my experience they work better too. I use a ringbacked notebook to list the things I have to do and use a coloured highlighter on the crucial items. The forty or so telephone numbers I use regularly are at the back, and all the others are on index cards. I only have to look at one page to see what I must do and that way I don't miss anything. A business acquaintance of mine has one of the complicated formal ones. At our first meeting she promised to do three things for me, wrote them down in three different places in her magic file – and didn't do any of them.

Moral – if you use them right, the simplest tricks work. If you don't bother to use them at all, no matter how superior they are, they are a total waste of money.

One final area you must give some thought to before you open the doors for business is that of security. You won't be too vulnerable to theft in a room at home (though personal computers are ever so nickable) but you could lose a lot of valuable paperwork if you become a victim of a domestic burglar who throws things around and tears things up in spite. In a rented office, you might suffer the same damage as well as stolen machinery and furniture wrecked in the search for a cash box.

But as soon as you open any sort of shop you will be considered fair game, both by the criminal fraternity and by opportunist customers. So before you order stock, make your plans for thwarting them. Insurance premiums are lower in country areas because the risks are smaller – organised criminals rarely venture far from urban areas and there are fewer drug addicts desperate for the price of their next fix. On the other hand, the country does have its own unsavoury characters, and if your stock is something valuable and easily resellable, like antiques, the 'rings' may decide to pay you a visit.

Wherever you are located, you can reduce your premium by fitting locks and burglar alarms of a type approved by your insurance company. What they like best is a 'central station' alarm, which activates a signal in the police station as well as making a noise on your premises. Another version telephones the police station and plays a pre-recorded tape which says, 'This is Bloggs Gift Shop in Station Road. We have intruders on the premises.'

Most of these sytems are electronic and respond to noise, vibration, movement or body heat, so they do not need the elaborate wiring of the older types and are therefore much cheaper to install. They are run on batteries or mains (or a combination) and any tampering with the control box sets them off. They also have a delay built in, so you have time to get out of the shop after switching on. Normal practice is to have at least one visible alarm box (or dummy) situated outside where it will deter passing opportunists. You will have to pay an annual maintenance charge as well as an installation fee; you may be able to buy this system outright and install it yourself but be sure this is acceptable to the insurance company. Another alarm system which might appeal to you is the sort which is actually tethered to valuable items; anyone trying to remove these items without the key trips off the alarm. You have probably seen them in furriers or hi-fi shops.

How much you need to do to the front of the shop depends on its location and its contents. In a well lit thoroughfare with plenty of passing traffic you shouldn't need to do much beyond fitting an obvious dead-lock to the front door – Yale-type locks are too easily opened by a determined thief. In less populated areas, or with a tempting stock of cigarettes or booze, it will be worth investing in a retractable grille. In either case, you should leave the shop lights on overnight so that intruders are visible to passers-by.

Tills should be left open at night and situated so that anyone looking through the window can see they are empty. Side or back doors and windows and sky-lights need dead-locks, bolts and obvious strong bars or grilles. Get them fixed to the inside so they cannot be removed by a thief with a screwdriver, and to the frame of the window, not the opening part, or a thief will just break the glass and open the window.

If your back yard is dark and inviting, think of a chained dog in a kennel by the door. But do not leave a vicious dog loose in the yard or the shop overnight, for this is illegal. Anyway, in the shop a dog would negate your alarm system. Don't let your big dog wander about the shop during the day, either. It will be off-putting to strangers and prevent regular customers combining 'walkies' with a buying trip.

One nasty type of theft is by staff. They can develop a 'she can afford it and she doesn't pay me very much' attitude. They might take items home with them to sell to friends, but they are more likely to fiddle what they ring up on the till (so have the sort of till where the customer can see what's rung up). Or they will have a couple of pounds out of the till every day and try to disguise it with overrings and underrings. Anyone who consistently makes a mess of their till-handling is probably doing it deliberately, so beware.

But the real problem is the innocent-seeming people who come into your shop during the day. Forget all that nonsense about emotionally disturbed menopausal women who shop-lift on the spur of the moment – shop-lifting is *theft* and it is deliberate. Most of the culprits come into your shop with the sole and express intention of stealing something. Watch strangers carefully, but don't trust people you know either, especially groups of children. They often have a rehearsed routine of a mock fight to distract your attention while small items are pocketed. Many vulnerable shops have an 'only one in the shop at a time' rule.

What you must understand is the difference between the honest mentality and the criminal mentality. When an honest person sees a vulnerable situation, say a wallet left on the counter, their reaction is to say, 'Whose is this?' The criminally inclined think, 'I could have that – can I get away with it?' So you must make sure they can't by keeping all the vulnerable items as inaccessible as possible. I don't mean just cheap small items like sweets and pencils, but big valuable ones too. I remember being told of a saddle that went from the launch party of a big new tack shop in London. The owner said, 'I saw it go – a man walked in the door, went straight to it, picked it up and walked out with it. There was nothing I could do about it – there were so many people in the shop I couldn't get to him.'

Your best defence against pickers-up of unconsidered trifles when the shop is open is to arrange your displays in such a way that people cannot disappear from sight behind them – and be sure that there is always an assistant in the shop and in sight. If it is not possible to arrange the displays to avoid dead-spots, some strategically placed mirrors will help you to keep an eye on people. Best of all is a closed-circuit TV system. Its main value is as a deterrent, so the monitor sets and cameras must be immediately visible; notices stating that the shop is protected this way also help. You rent these systems on a weekly basis.

For firms that deal with this, burglar alarms and all other aspects of security, look in the *Yellow Pages* under 'Security'. These firms will also help with the selection and installation of safes. You should have one, for it is prudent to make a point of removing large-denomination notes from the till at regular intervals. The best type is the 'hole in the floor' sort where you have a little hole to poke notes through, for then you only have to unlock and open the safe when you are ready to go to the bank. Put cheques and credit card receipts in it as well, for although they are less at risk than cash, they might be snatched from the till with a handful of notes.

I've already said that for the sake of your overdraft you should go to the bank every day. You should do it for the sake of security also, for a determined thief will get into your safe one way or another. They might rip it out of the wall or floor, or they might decide it is easier to beat you into opening it for them.

Go to the bank yourself. It is not fair to get a member of staff to do it unless you are very small and you can send a large male. From the day you open (and particularly in the early weeks, for this is when you are most likely to be observed for your 'easy job' potential) vary your route to the bank, vary the time you go and, if you can, vary your vehicle. Don't walk about with obvious bank books and money in your hand. Put it in different bags, preferably shopping bags. Open a Giro account and pay cash into that, either all the time if there is a post office closer than the bank, or part of the time as a variation in your routine. You can then pay a Giro cheque into your bank. Your insurance covers you for cash in transit to the bank as well as on your premises.

Arrange to use the bank's nightsafe, so you can get money off your premises at weekends, bank holidays or late in the afternoon. You pay a small fee and the bank gives you a key to the nightsafe and some leather pouches to put the money in. The pouches also lock and you are the only person with a key to them. So you go into the bank when it is open, ask for your pouch, open it up and pay in as usual.

Pay staff wages by cheque. It saves you the chore of making up the right amount of cash, it reduces the risks of keeping cash on the premises, it simplifies your accounts – and with luck it leaves the money in your bank a little longer, while the cheque is cleared!

7 Moving the goods

Let's get one thing clear before we go any further. Whether you call them customers or clients, your business needs people to buy its goods and services, and if *you* don't treat them right, they will buy from someone else. You may think that is so obvious it doesn't need saying, but at least once a week I come across a shop or organisation that doesn't deserve to stay in business. It's not just the amateurish fumblings I mentioned in the last chapter, or failure to keep promises, it is frequently downright bloodymindedness.

Examples are the local food shop whose owner, in front of a large queue of other customers, rudely insisted she wanted my address as well as cheque guarantee card (I left nearly £50 worth of goods on the counter and walked out never to return), the man in the electrical goods shop who couldn't be bothered to put his mug of tea down and show us extractor fans (we walked out of that shop too), or, worst of all, the organisations who didn't bother to ring me back or send me the information I asked for when researching this book. You will find none of those in the appendices – writing is a business, too, and I do not recommend people unless I know they are good.

These people all seem to be labouring under the misapprehension that they are entitled to make a living without any more effort than putting up an 'open for business' sign. Others think they are entitled to make their full percentage profit on every item they stock. This sort take it as a personal insult if you ask for a discount on bulk buys, instead of seeing it as a windfall extra sale, or if you have the temerity to return faulty goods to them.

They are all busily upsetting customers, presumably assuming that there will always be plenty more. The sad fact of the matter is that for virtually every purchase a customer might want to make there is a big chain store ready to supply it. People shop at little places because they are handy, but if they are also run by bloody-minded people the customers will get in their cars and go along to Safeway or Payless or whoever, where the service may be impersonal but is at least courteous, and where returns are never questioned and the selection is much larger.

In a retail situation you must start by making sure you know what your customers want to buy and how much they are prepared to pay for it. Once you are established and know some of them well enough, there is a surprisingly simple way to find out this information – you ask! 'I was thinking of stocking some rubber gloves, Mrs Jones. Would they be any use to you? They'd be about £1 a pair' should bring a definite response.

You will have a fair idea of the sort of things you want to sell before you even find your premises, but you must refine this idea a great deal before you order stock. You won't sell Bethnal Green goods in Bond Street any more than you will get Bond Street prices in Bethnal Green. Another thing you must not try to do is impose your own taste on people. One failed gents' outfitter complained bitterly, 'I had beautiful quality suits, but all they wanted was denim jeans,' and couldn't see that he was the one who was wrong.

It is well worth spending some time driving round your new location and making some detailed observations of the dwellings, the cars and the people themselves, especially at the times when they come and go from work. Remember that rashes of estate agents' boards, skips and scaffolding means the area is moving upmarket, but don't expect it to get there overnight. Upmarket does mean better quality goods, but it also means that the customers are more mobile. If they don't think your quality justifies your prices, they'll hop back in their cars and go away. If your offering is high quality and has any sort of rarity value, and you're not charging a high price for it, you're an idiot.

Resale price maintenance is no longer with us, and with the exception of a few items, like books, all the manufacturers can do is suggest a 'Recommended Resale Price' (RRP). With such goods, how closely you stick to that RRP is up to you, after due consideration on what the competition charges and how easy it is for customers to get to them. With items that do not have either of these constraints, you charge what the market will bear. That is also dependent upon the competition, but if your product is really unique and desirable it becomes 'price insensitive'. This means it will sell at any price, and you might as well make the most of it while you can.

Incidentally, if what you are selling relates to a sport or hobby, do not fall into the trap of giving the local enthusiasts' club members a discount. 10 per cent is the usual amount, and it makes a big hole in your profit. There is no need to do it, anyway. If your stock is right and the general level of your prices is right and you are conveniently situated, they will buy from you anyway. Unless someone is buying in bulk and makes it clear that they will only do so if you give a discount, don't. Even in this situation, don't do it unless the sale leaves you with enough stock to satisfy your regular customers (at the full price) until you can get a delivery.

On the other hand, if someone offers you a reduced price in cash for a big item that you've had in stock for a long time, don't miss the chance of getting rid of it by being too stubborn. Haggle a bit, by all means, but remember that as long as you get back its cost, plus a little more than the interest cost for the time you've had it, you've made a true profit. Which means that you must have stock records of a sort that allow you to check quickly and easily how long you've had things and how much you paid for them. You cannot possibly keep this sort of thing in your head accurately.

Nor, without proper records, can you evaluate the profitability of various items. You must include the interest element in your pricing, especially with slow sellers whose manufacturers will not 'break bulk' and insist you have a boxful.

You also need those records to help you establish a pattern of seasonal sales, and to help you with re-ordering. People don't buy anti-freeze for their cars in July, but if they do start buying in October and it has a four-month delivery period, you need to order in June. It is not unreasonable to assume that you will sell the same quantities in each month as last year, but without proper records how are you going to know what those quantities were, and arrange deliveries accordingly? There is no point in paying for a whole season's stock in one go if you don't have to.

You must do a full stock-take at the year-end, so your stock can be reflected accurately in your accounts. If you have a big shop, lots of stock and several members of staff, you should do it more frequently and insist on all sales being recorded by a stock number, as a safeguard against light fingers. Best of all, maintain a running stock-check as part of your re-ordering and display systems.

The simplest way of keeping your stock records is on cards. You can buy them ready ruled from stationers or buy blanks and rule them up yourself. You need the description and your stock number on the top line, and columns for purchase dates and costs, VAT, numbers sold (or 'missing') and the number currently in stock. You can put the supplier's name and catalogue number on the back.

Whatever you sell, you will need to display it, so you will need some shop fittings. If you sell any form of clothing you will want somewhere for customers to try it on and you will need a biggish mirror situated so they can get a long view of themselves. You will also need some clothing rails and some shelves. Most other items will go on shelves, or you will find the manufacturers' reps will recommend special display stands. They may even give you some if they are anxious enough for you to take the stock. You can buy all sorts of beautiful display stands from specialists, but the more beautiful they are, the more expensive. You can also buy them second-hand. What you can get away with is entirely dependent on your market positioning.

Where you get your main stock from is not likely to be a problem. Place an advert in the trade journals to announce your opening date and you will be besieged by reps and catalogues. If there is not too much price variation, you may do better buying from a wholesaler than straight from manufacturers. The wholesaler will have goods from several manufacturers for you to choose from, with all of whom they have much more clout than you do as an individual. You will also have one delivery, one invoice and one accounting entry to make instead of half a dozen, and in many trades the rep will have a van full of stock for you to take on the spot. They will also have a better idea of what will sell in your part of the country than a distant manufacturer.

Once you've been trading for a while, you will get to know where to get supplies at the best prices. If your turnover is big enough, you may be able to get items specially packaged or made to your design. Just don't expect competitors to tell you where to go for this. They will rightly consider this information to be their own trade secret.

One other place you might be able to get stock from is 'bankrupt stock' auctions. You do need to know exactly what stuff would cost elsewhere and ruthlessly stick to your limit price for each lot. And you have to make two or three trips to the auction room – one to view, one to bid and maybe another to collect. That said, you can pick up some real bargains. I've seen our local auction sell off the stock from a motorbike shop, a garden centre, several small grocers, several wine bars, umpteen cheap dress shops and many others.

If you deal in a speciality, auctions are also a good source of second-hand items. I include antiques under this heading (not *lèse majesté* – they are stock and you can't get them from the manufacturers. Er – yes you can. Just don't let your customers find out!) but mostly these items will relate to sports or hobbies.

Once you are known to deal in such items you will find customers will want to trade their old equipment in against new, while others will bring stuff to you because they want to get rid of it. There are a couple of advantages here. One is that people come a long way to see your second-hand stock, then decide they'd rather have new and buy it from you while they're there. The other is that it is normal practice with used goods to sell them for the owner on a commission, which means you have no outlay and only pay VAT on the commission. If you actually buy stuff to sell, you have to pay VAT on the whole of the sale price, often without an invoice that allows a VAT deduction on the purchase price.

If you do buy second-hand items, naturally you do not pay very much for them, for they are not as easy to sell as new, and you may have to keep them a long time. Finally, you must be very certain that the items you are buying are not stolen and that you get receipts (with addresses) for each item.

Whether the goods you are selling are new or used, you are still bound by the Sale of Goods Acts. The important bits are these. Firstly, goods must be of 'merchantable quality', which basically means that they mustn't fall apart. Next, they must be 'fit for the purpose for which they are intended' which is to a certain extent self-explanatory, but includes the fact that a customer is entitled to rely on *your* 'professional skill and judgement', so if they have asked for your recommendations, you'd better be right. In practical terms it means that if the goods are not right, you take them back and refund the money. But it could also mean your being sued for damages if the goods have been the cause of an accident, so check your insurance policy. Incidentally, since *you* sold the goods, *you* carry the can, not the manufacturer or wholesaler, although obviously you can expect them to replace faulty items.

This whole area of specialities does require that you have a thorough knowledge of your subject. Most of your customers will be enthusiasts and they will soon detect your ignorance and put it into the relevant grapevine. You must be up to date with it too, then you may be able to detect a sub-trend and slant your stock in that direction. For instance, some years ago it became the rage among the horsey set to ride cowboy-style. There were demonstration teams and special competitions at all the shows and a couple of switched-on saddlers made some nice extra money by stocking those saddles and bridles as well as their ordinary stuff.

They also did a roaring trade in mail order, which is another sales outlet for the specialist. There are plenty of enthusiasts living in remote areas who cannot easily get to a shop, so have no option but to buy their supplies through the post. Selling this way, you have to budget for continuous advertising, packaging materials, 'goods in transit' insurance, postage or carriage charges, the inevitable returns and possibly the production, updating and printing of a catalogue. Unless you are only offering a few easily listed items, you must decide between large and expensive advertisements or some form of catalogue or price list.

The more elaborate this is, the more the production costs. Don't even think of colour photographs unless you are sure you are going to sell hundreds of items – no printer will produce such a brochure in small quantities and your initial outlay will be enormous. You will also need somewhere to store the catalogues. It is normal to ask for payment for the catalogues ('Send £2 for catalogue'), but then to deduct that payment from the first order.

Whether you list all your wares or offer a catalogue, no magazine will accept your advertisements until you sign their form guaranteeing that you will comply with the rules of their 'mail order protection scheme'. The form is long, and legalistic, but it basically concerns the quality of the goods, requires you to operate a 'return goods, money back' guarantee and insists you specify the waiting period between receipt of cash and delivery of goods.

Most companies say 'Allow twenty-eight days for delivery', which means you don't even have to order the goods from your suppliers until you have sold them – and been paid by your customers! Obviously this will only work if your supplier can guarantee you a short delivery time, but if you find you are selling a lot of whatever-it-is, you can always threaten to find a new, more cooperative supplier, not to mention one who will give you a good bulk discount.

Even without the twenty-eight day rule, you do not send the goods until the customer's cheque has been cleared. With credit cards, this problem does not arise. I was told by one retailer that their mail order sales increased dramatically when they started taking credit card telephone orders (don't forget you need an additional agreement to do this). Put yourself in the customer's place – no forms to fill in, no letter to write and post, just pick up a telephone. You can even talk to someone about the thing you want, to ask if it is suitable.

Of course, mail order is not confined to specialists. You only have to look at the clothing advertisements in the daily and Sunday papers to see that. If you do think of that market, be prepared for a very high volume of responses. I read recently of one dress manufacturer who decided to try mail order and placed her advertisement in one of the Sunday colour supplements. She had over 12,000 replies.

Don't confuse mail order with direct mail. With mail order you advertise and say 'buy this item' or 'send for catalogue'. With direct mail, you send out catalogues on spec and hope the recipients will buy. You will probably be aware that lists of names are saleable – if you've ever bought anything by mail order yourself, or sent for a brochure, you will have received catalogues for similar goods in the mail.

You buy your lists of potential customers from a broker, by socio-economic and interest classification, or you get them to do the mail-shot for you. They prefer the latter, as it means you don't see the list and so can't use it again without paying them. Since they themselves farm out the job of stuffing and despatching the envelopes, they will allow you to give them a few names and addresses of your own so you can check the stuff really is posted and that it arrives in good condition.

You should insist on being credited for all returned letters – they are supposed to have sold you an up-to-date list, not an old inaccurate one. Then you wait for the orders to come in, but I must warn you that 2 per cent is considered the normal response rate. It isn't a cheap exercise, either. The names cost about 10p each, and that's before you pay for the catalogue printing and the postage. Which is why it is normal to use treble the cost of the goods as a selling price.

On the subject of addresses, there is no reason why you should not sell your customers to a list broker to gain a few extra pennies. Even if you do not do this, it is always useful to have a list of regulars, as you can then send them an invitation to view your new season's stock. I've been asked to put my address on an envelope for this purpose by a dress shop, and asked to put it on a sticky label at a herb farm for their next catalogue. No one is offended if you ask 'Would you like . . .?'

But how do you get them into your shop in the first place? I don't mean the passing trade, but the other sort, who won't find you if you don't make some effort to let them know you're there. The best value for money spent on advertising for this purpose is in local newspapers, but if you handle it right, you should be able to get some free editorial coverage.

Local newspapers are interested in local events and local people, so you have a double advantage if you have lived in the district any length of time. You can even tell the readers what a splendid person you are under the guise of a potted life history. Rather like preparing a CV to send to prospective employers, you play up the good bits and keep quiet about the rest. 'Betty Bloggs has lived in Blanktown for the last six months after spending most of her life in Grungeshire where she is well known in the running fraternity for her enthusiasm in supporting local mini-marathons [you don't mention that you've never finished the course]. She is now applying her expertise for the benefit of the sportswomen of Blanktown by opening a Sports Clothes shop in Station Road.'

You can do this in two ways. You can either telephone the paper, tell them when you are going to open and ask if they'd like to send a reporter, or you put your PR hat on and send out a proper press release (headed 'press release') with the story ready written and a couple of captioned photographs of you in your jogging suit. The paper will probably suggest that you place an advertisement on the same page as their editorial. Don't – people will assume the whole thing is an advertisement placed by you and that reduces its value.

Do keep sending the press releases, with captioned photographs, every time you do something that constitutes good copy. You ought to get a mention a couple of times a year this way, especially if you remember that a lot of things that seem old hat to you could be an interesting novelty to the editor – 'A team from the Blanktown Harriers has entered for the Grungeshire Amateur Athletic Association's Cross-Country Championships. Betty Bloggs of The Sports Clothes Shop says, "They are a good team and stand every chance of winning. I'm proud to have supplied their equipment." ' (Incidentally, do send copies of your press releases to your local radio station. They are less likely to use them than the papers, but you might be lucky.)

Although you shouldn't advertise on the same page as your editorial features, there is no reason why you shouldn't advertise in the local paper on a regular basis if the rates are right. The cheapest way is to do it for a specified period of several weeks. The acknowledged best places are the front or back pages, and although these are obviously in high demand you might be able to bring down the price per insertion if you do it for a long enough period.

One of the snags of specialising is that you will be approached to sponsor classes at local events. Sponsorship is considered to be advertising for accounting purposes, but it is not always cost effective. You will only get a mention in the programme in the general text, where for the cost of the prize money for one class, you could have a full-page advertisement on the back of the programme.

The best idea I've encountered on this theme is to present vouchers, redeemable for goods in your shop. Twenty £5 vouchers don't even cost you £100 – they cost the wholesale price of £100 worth of goods. And then only if each winner bothers to come and use it, and takes an item selling for exactly £5. Most wait until they need something (during which time you have had the use of the money) and will then spend much more than £5. If they have come from outside your usual catchment area, so much the better.

Just be sure you make them welcome and encourage them to come back – and bring their friends.

8 Selling skills

Retailing is a happy situation, for your customers come to you preconditioned to buy. In all other situations, you have to go to the customers and persuade them to buy. You certainly do in the early days, and even when you are an established name the times when a customer approaches you with cheque book in hand are very rare.

One way of tackling this problem, if you have actual goods to sell, is to use agents. Certainly if you want to cover a major part of the country this is a cheaper way to do it than to employ your own sales force. They will have many useful contacts, will already be known to and trusted by their existing customers, and will, once they have accepted you as worthwhile, be a good source of information on what the competition is up to. (This works both ways!)

You can find them in the *Yellow Pages* under 'manufacturers agents', and I should perhaps add here that you can consult a full set of *Yellow Pages* for the whole country at main post offices or public libraries (in the reference section). Alternatively, advertise for these agents in the trade press, specifying which areas you want to cover.

Before you actually appoint agents, you will want to take up references with their other clients and ask some detailed questions about their experience of your type of product. They will be self-employed (or their employer won't know what they are up to, which could lead to complications) and the way you pay them is a matter for mutual negotiation. Some work on a straight commission basis, in which case you will need to set some sort of minimum sales targets so you can get rid of them if they don't perform. Others prefer to act as wholesalers. You don't have to have the same arrangement with all of them, but you do need to set geographical boundaries, for they will all want to know exactly where their territory is.

Without agents to sell your goods, and in all other situations, you will have to polish up your own selling skills. And I do mean *selling*, not just order-taking. There is a popular myth that a good product will practically sell itself, but if you believe that you will have your share of rejections earlier than most.

Rejection is part of the seller's lot and it is something you will have to learn to cope with. The trick is to realise that it is not you personally that the buyer is rejecting, nor the fact that you are a woman. It is that many people regard selling as an intrusion and react appropriately unless you get your approach right. It may well be that you are approaching the wrong people, by which I do not mean that you should write to the chief buyer rather than the managing director, although of course you should. You may be aiming at the wrong target altogether, if you didn't research your market properly.

It isn't that difficult to get the information you need. If you don't feel you can tackle it on your own, tell the Institute of Marketing what you need and they will consult their register of marketing consultants for a selection of suitable experts. This is not a free or even a subsidised service, and you may, after you have enquired about fees, decide you would rather do it yourself after all.

There are plenty of sources of information. The Department of Trade and Industry produces quarterly 'Business Monitors' which report on the quantity and value of trade in various areas. The Small Firms Service has a booklet on tendering for government contracts. The Central Statistical

Office produces a series of reports, including the Registrar General's annual report on size and age range of local populations and the 'Family Expenditure Survey' which details spending on specific items. There are many other surveys produced commercially, so keep your eye on the trade journals.

Look at them all and see if you can determine a pattern which will be useful to you. Allow your intuition to help, but don't make the mistake of confusing what you think you know with what you really do know. Don't allow your natural partiality for your product to blind you into ignoring the signs that should lead to a change of direction. Just because a product has always sold well for other people in the past doesn't mean it will do for you now, or ever. Some markets are finite, and you may have had your brilliant idea just too late.

One of the jargon words much used in marketing circles is 'positioning'. It could equally be expressed as marksmanship, or the art of accurately setting your sights on a specific target – the rifle rather than the shotgun. In the small business context, shotgun ammunition is too costly.

So, it's down to some carefully planned advertisements in the trade press and some equally carefully planned sales literature. As a general principle, the object of this exercise is to get your name in front of your target audience, so they know who you are when they get your pre-approach letter in the post. Blow your trumpet about how brilliant you are, but keep it brief, keep it simple and don't try to be too clever. I promise you, every gimmick you might think of has long since been milked to death and none of them will advance your cause.

It is not difficult to find out who your letters should be addressed to. There are plenty of directories available, classified by trade or company size or whatever, with all the senior management listed by title and name. The best of these are the 'Kompass' directories, particularly their Regional Sales Guides.

If what you want to know isn't in a directory, just pick up a telephone and ask. 'I need to write to the head of your buying/data processing/personnel department. Would you give me his name please? Is he in that office?' They will tell you all that, and the title he uses, and how he spells his name. Whatever you do, make sure you get that right. It is a dreadful insult to spell a name wrong – usefully so if you want to needle someone in the build-up to litigation, but the death-knell of your chances of getting in front of the person you want to see in any other situation.

You won't sell them anything unless you get in front of them and you won't get there unless that first letter is right. Don't use it for your sales pitch, you want to do that yourself. Don't go into any great detail at all – busy people don't have time to read long letters. Senior people don't read any letters at all unless their secretary thinks they should, so word it in a way that makes sure they are shown it for a decision.

Dear Mr Higgins, I am sure you will have seen our advertisements in the *Widget Makers' Gazette*. I feel sure our service will be of interest to you and would like the opportunity of presenting it to you myself. I have an appointment in Yourtown next Thursday morning, but will be free in the early afternoon. I will telephone your secretary next week to confirm a time.
Your sincerely,
Eloisa J. Bloggs.

That isn't an 'Oh please can I come and see you?' letter, it's an 'I'm a busy person like you and I can fit you in next week.

Don't miss it, it might be important to you' letter and it stands a fair chance of getting you ten minutes of the man's time. That is all you want at this stage. You want your chance to suss the man out on his home ground to see how he ticks, so you know how to angle your detailed approach. You also want him to see you. People will not do business with someone they don't like, which is why the Golden Rule of selling is 'sell yourself before you try to sell the product'.

The rules of selling yourself are the same as for any other product. The first one is that the packaging has got to be right, or the buyer won't bother to look inside. In other words, you have got to be dressed in a way that makes you credible to the buyer. Unless it really is your body you are selling, remember that what you are trying to convey is a competent business-like image, not a feminine frivolous sexy one. This means you must avoid frills, high skirts, low necks, bare arms or back, overtight items and faddy extremes of fashion.

Avoid items that will distract the audiences' attention from what you are saying, such as clattering bangles or earrings that hang and bob – and keep your breasts under control. A good bra is essential to keep them from moving around and to conceal the nipples. Many men are embarrassed by jiggling breasts and protruberant nipples, but some will interpret erect nipples as a sign that you fancy them. Don't forget that nipples automatically erect when you are tense or excited, either of which can apply in a selling situation.

For the same reason, don't cross your legs when you sit. This tends to give a good view up your skirt and you will inevitably want to uncross or recross them, which could be interpreted as flashing your thighs.

Don't go to the other extreme and dress too much like a man. It doesn't give you authority, it is seen either as cute or as an indication that you are a lesbian. This will not endear you to male buyers, and although most women will not think of it, you may come across a/nother lesbian. I have no experience of this world, so cannot advise you, but I feel sure it will lead to complications rather than a sale. Anyway, no male-type trouser suits and no men's ties. These are regarded as a penis symbol – and if you choose pink or red, you've really got it wrong.

Another item to avoid is real fur, either a full coat or trimmings. You have no way of telling beforehand (unless the name of the organisation tells you, like Greenpeace) whether your audience might have ecological or emotional objections to humans wearing animal fur and you could be shown the door rapidly without knowing why.

Other than that, and the fact that you should be neat and tidy with low-key makeup, the precise style of what you wear should be dependant on where you are going. Modify your personal preferences to the likely socio-economic background of your audience. There is a world of difference between Wardour Street in London and Factory Lane in Bolton. What will be approved in one will be sniffed at or laughed at in the other.

The final thought about clothes for selling in is that they have to be geared to the fact that you will be getting in and out of cars, going in and out of offices which may not be that clean, carrying a briefcase or presentation kit, and possibly bending and stretching while you do that presentation. So go for fabrics that do not crease or stain or pick up fluff and that fall back into place on their own. You want to arrive at your appointment looking unflustered and you want to be able to stay that way, not have to keep fussing at your clothes.

The whole object of this exercise is to tell your audience what you want them to know about you, without letting them know too much about how you tick. That's what you want to know about them.

So the first thing you do, as soon as you get into the building, is to take in how it is laid out, how it is furnished, and the general demeanour of the workers. Does the atmosphere change as you get closer to the great man's office? Does the standard of furnishing? These things will give you an indication of how he sees himself and his subordinates and where he is likely to put you in his scale of importance.

It is well known in sales circles that some buyers are absolute pigs, making the most of every opportunity to wield their power. They make you wait for hours in dingy uncomfortable waiting-rooms and then are rude when they do condescend to see you. If you are anxious to sell your goods, there is not a lot you can do about this except put up with it.

It shouldn't be like this when you are selling a service. You will be dealing with a professional in your own line, who will assume you know your business, but this does not mean they won't use all the little power ploys to subtly put you down. Even professionals can suffer from feelings of inadequacy and need to indulge in opportunities to boost their ego. They may see you as a threat to their comfortable security or they may just be softening you up for the kill at price-fixing time.

On the whole, you will be much less likely to encounter this sort of nonsense from women. Most of them are not in the office to play power politics, they are there to get a job done. Their interest in you will be whether you are as good at your job as they are at theirs, and whether you can offer them something to aid them in getting that job done.

If you find you are suffering a lot of put-downs, or you have too many meetings that end with a 'Don't call us . . .' and you are sure your product is right, it may be that you need to go on an assertiveness training course. These courses make you do a lot of role-playing exercises to help you feel your way through difficult situations without being too submissive or too aggressive. They will also help you work your way through your own particular hang-ups.

A potential situation that worries a lot of women is the man who says, 'I'll buy from you if you'll go to bed with me.' It probably won't happen to you, but you should have your response ready, just in case. I have always reckoned that if I was closer to the door than he was, I would pack my briefcase, say, 'I don't want to do that. I'm sorry we can't do business,' and depart. If he was between me and the door, I would fling the contents of his desk at him or on the floor and make a dash for the door. But I'm sure you know how to deal with randy men as well as I do – most of us have been practising since we were about fourteen!

Back to dealing with people rather than reacting to the way they treat you. The object of the exercise, you will recall, is to get your message across, and even if you haven't given it any great thought you must be aware that different people process information in different ways. The simplest version of this is that they are either readers or listeners.

A reader likes to have information in a form that he can look at. A listener likes to be told. The reader won't let you go into details on the telephone, he'll ask you to write, and he will prefer to deal with queries by letter, whereas the listener will happily talk to you on the telephone, or respond to your offer of brochures by asking you to come and tell him about it.

There is more to it than this, and it is worth considering if you want to get the best from your opportunities to communicate. Most of us favour one of our senses over the others in the way we perceive things. We are predominantly thinkers, visualisers, listeners or feelers and if you present us with a piece of information, we will deal with it in our favoured way. We will assimilate it more readily if you present it in terms that appeal to our favoured sense. This is why you need to observe your audience closely and modify your approach accordingly.

Thinkers will listen to you, shut their eyes and apply logic to what you have said, working through all the possibilities before they give their carefully considered answers. They respond well if you use words like 'logically' and 'precisely', ask them 'What do you think?' or tell them 'I would value your opinion.'

Visualisers can be detected by their use of phrases like 'I see' or 'That's not quite clear' even before they go into their routine of converting everything you say into pictures to compare with the visual records in their head. This tends to involve tensing the neck muscles and gazing at the ceiling, or into middle distance. Don't interfere with this by placing yourself at their point of focus or trying to meet their eyes. Put them at their ease by saying 'I'd like to show you' or 'How does it look to you?'

Hearers may have evidence of a love of music in their offices, or may be detected by their melodious and rhythmic speech patterns. It is important to them that things should sound good, so do not upset them with loud speech, or dropped briefcases while they are holding a silent conversation with themselves over the pros and cons of your presentation. Ask 'Does that sound OK?' or 'Does it ring any bells with you?'

Feelers are interested in sensation. They like to be surrounded by things that are nice to handle and will probably help you into a chair and lay a hand on your arm to check the texture of your sleeve. They have 'feelie' toys on their desk and will handle these or their own clothes, which will be of beautiful tactile material. They wriggle a lot, too, because they like the way it feels and respond well to suggestions that you can help them 'Get to grips' with their problems, or 'Put them in touch' with the answers.

If you come across one who is into flavours or aromas (the former will probably be overweight, the latter will breathe in your smell as you come into the room or comment on your perfume) you will endear yourself to him by commenting on a local restaurant and how marvellous it smelt as you passed.

Don't annoy slow talkers by gabbling or slow breathers by panting. Don't talk slowly to fast talkers or they'll think you are thick – but do breathe slowly to calm down the excitable, even if you have to breathe at his fast rate for a while before slowing down gradually. Don't make a big display of it or he'll think you are taking the mickey. But it works, as I proved many times on the back seats of cars in my youth!

And watch their eyes all the time. It is an involuntary reflex, when interested in something, for the eyebrows to raise and the pupils to dilate – it widens the eyes so you can see better. If you see it in your audience, you'll know you've got a good chance and you can press home your attack. It cannot be controlled, only hidden by dark glasses or disguised as a response to light conditions. It is the reason many buyers (and other players of power games) situate their desks so that they have their backs to the window. You have to squint to see them at all; they are looking into a darker interior which makes their pupils wide anyway and that makes it that much more difficult to see a reaction to your presentation.

As well as being a most important part of your feedback system, this reflex is your final weapon in the fight to get people interested in you and your product. Reverse the calming-down process above by matching your breathing to that of the person you are talking to, then encourage them to speed it up to excitement level, look into their eyes and widen your own as you deliver your punch line.

Obviously all this works best on a one-to-one basis. If you find yourself presenting your case to a group of people, work out which are the most important and try, very subtly, to work out what makes them tick. I say very subtly, because otherwise you may alienate some of the others in the process, and they will queer your pitch for you when you've gone.

Although you should be able to read the feedback as you talk, and modify your presentation accordingly, do not let yourself be chivvied into missing bits. Stick to your planned logical order, and delay dealing with arguments or objections until the end, or you may not be able to pick up the thread again. If you have visual aids or samples, keep them to yourself until the right moment. You want people to listen to you, not play with samples or wonder what you have in the display case.

For heaven's sake enthuse about your product or service. If you don't sound as though you think it's marvellous, you will never convince anyone else. Most important of all, learn when to shut up. More sales have been lost by idiots babbling to fill a void, while the buyer is making up his mind, than from any other cause.

All that is left to do at that stage is to haggle over the price. Perhaps we had better call it negotiating, for haggling implies that the only point at issue is money, which is by no means the case. If that were all, it would be as easy as pricing in a retail situation – 'I've got the goods, I want £X for them because they cost me £Y and my profit mark-up is Z per cent.' Here the situation is one that involves an infinite set of variables, whether it is bulk goods or a stretch of someone's time or brain power.

If it is goods, who pays for delivery, insurance, breakages, return cost of rejects? Who decides what constitutes a reject? How are they to be packed – number per carton, cartons per crate/container? What is the cost of packaging to the customer's design? Where do they want them? When? All at once or in batches over a long/short period? How will they pay – instalments, on delivery thirty/forty-five/sixty days later? Will they pay more for an exclusive dealership?

If it is services, how many people do they want and for how long? When? What level of seniority? Your place or theirs? Who pays for travel, accommodation, food? How many meals a day? Who provides necessary machinery, stationery, secretarial assistance? Do they get exclusive rights to the results of all this work, or can you sell it to someone else? When will they pay – at the end, or will there be some interim payment?

All of this means you must have done your homework. You must know exactly what everything costs, including money, for don't forget you have to finance it all (remember about over-trading?). You must know the availability of materials and people, where you can sub-contract and what that will cost.

You must know what is the norm in the industry, in all the possible situations. You must have a pretty good idea what competitors would charge; whether any of them, and which ones, might be bidding against you; and whether they have the capacity available to produce the goods in the time. You should know how you are rated in comparison with those competitors, whether your expertise is unique and how long it would take someone else to acquire it.

And last, but by no means least, you should know whether you want a big one-off profit or a long-term relationship with each customer.

9 Managing your time and your life

When you are managing a small business, there are a million and forty-nine things to be done and only so many hours in a day to do them. It is especially difficult to adjust if you have just left a full-time job to start your own business. When you have nobody to account to but yourself, it is easy to spend your day being very busy without actually achieving anything.

Part of the problem is that you do not have an awareness of the value of your time – literally £s per hour. Before you do anything else, sit down and work this out (and do it again at regular intervals, for as your business builds, your worth will change). Divide the amount you are making per week by the number of hours you spend, and there's your answer.

If you find you could be making more by scrubbing floors, it is time to find out exactly how you spend your time now. It won't be easy, but try to list, day by day, for the last week, just what you did with each half hour when you were meant to be working. Be honest – there's no point in fooling yourself. If you were wasting time, list it. Make a list of all those activities, in order of the amount of time you spent on them, and then put that list aside. Then, on a clean sheet of paper, write down all the activities you feel you ought to be doing (whether or not you are) and reorganise this list in order of importance. Now compare this list of desirables with the list of actuals and the odds are you will get a nasty surprise at how much time you are spending on low-importance activities.

How many hours are you spending panicking because something has gone wrong? There is an old saying that goes

'When you are up to your neck in alligators, it is difficult to remember that your prime objective is to drain the swamp.' But a good drainage scheme is the only answer to the problem and the sooner you recognise it and take steps to organise one the better.

Suppose the thing that is taking all your time is going to the launderette because the washing machine keeps breaking down. This is taking, on average, three hours a week. You've just costed your time at £10 per hour, so your washing costs £30 a week. How many weeks' worth of your precious time will a new machine cost? This concept is known to economists as 'opportunity cost', but it's really only common sense, once you start costing your time.

What else is there on that list of activities that could be rationalised, or helped on its way by the right bit of equipment? Are you spending several hours laboriously typing repetitive letters when a word-processing bureau could do them more quickly and cheaply than your time-cost? If all they are are letters saying 'please send me your catalogue' why are you typing a letter when you could have handwritten those five words on a postcard printed with your trading name? Why are you typing addresses on envelopes when you could buy window envelopes?

The other side of rationalisation is the mental one – your ability to convince yourself that a time-wasting activity is worthwhile. One of the classic time-wasters is reading the newspapers every day – 'in case there is something relevant'. No doubt you should read relevant items, but the whole newspaper? There can be very few things that will need your immediate action to prevent disaster before they are fully reported in the trade magazines.

If you have to read technical books as well as trade magazines, you may be tempted to learn speed-reading. The principle behind it is that you should take in blocks of print, rather than read each word individually. This means you don't move your eyes across the page but straight down the middle. Your peripheral vision should take in everything up to the margins instead of being wasted on blank paper as it is when you scan back and forth. Train yourself with the aid of a timer. See how much you can read in ten minutes, then each day try to take in more in that time. It doesn't count if you don't take in what you have read, but you will find that your eye will latch on to significant words and alert you to the need for a little more attention to that passage.

Are there any regular tasks you do that don't really need doing at all? A lot of women tend to gild the lily on the basis of 'I like things to be nice' when it makes no real difference to the customers. Flowers are nice in a shop, but they are not what brings the customer through the door, and they take time that could be better spent.

Once you've weeded out all the things you don't need to do, you can concentrate on the jobs you should do and start thinking about priorities. If you have difficulty with this, remember that anything related to the past is history. Unless it is an official return or will prevent you being sued, it should have low priority. Items that will make a real difference to the future should always have precedence.

Get a fresh piece of paper and list all the jobs you have to do. Decide which are the really important ones and mark them A or TODAY. The not quite so desperate ones you mark B or TOMORROW, the next batch C or THIS WEEK and the rest Z or SOME TIME. The final job is to define the A list a little more by marking each task A1, A2, A3 etc. in order of priority. There is no need to do this with the B's or C's, as they either become A's or go away. Z's almost invariably do go away and here is one of the values of this system, in that by labelling a job as being of small importance, you won't waste your time in doing it.

If, instead of listing all your tasks, you prefer to organise them into piles, you can do so, or even jot each job down on a 3" by 5" file card. The important thing is to list each task as it comes to mind, because you can then forget it. No point in cluttering up your head with 'things to do' when you can let a piece of paper do it for you. The simplest method of doing all this is to keep a notebook for the purpose. Carry it with you at all times so it is handy for jotting things down when you think of them, then consult it every time you pause and wonder what to do next. As each job is completed, cross it off and move on to the next highest priority. Resist the urge to do C's because they are easy and can soon be crossed off your list.

Whenever the list gets untidy or difficult to read, just rewrite it. Do this at least once a day anyway, to refresh your mind and check your priorities. A good time to do this is first thing in the morning, when you have seen what is in your post and know if there is anything new that needs to be dealt with urgently. When you are fresh in the morning you are more likely to tackle a major task easily and less likely to be side-tracked. You will also have a new perspective on the tasks left over from yesterday and your subconscious may well have come up with the answer to one of yesterday's problems while you were asleep.

This often happens spontaneously, but you can take advantage of it by actually setting your brain a problem to deal with while you are asleep. The best method is a fairly casual 'Now what should I do about so and so?' rather than detailed concentration which is more likely to confuse the issue and keep you awake. Once you get into the habit of this you will find it frequently works and often produces a new angle that hadn't occurred to you before. But do take the precaution of keeping a notebook by your bed in case the answer comes at 3 a.m. and is gone again in the morning!

If you find this does work for you, you may prefer to make planning tomorrow's work your last job of the day, as part of your wind-down. If overnight answers don't alter the plan, you can start work on your designated first task in the morning before the contents of the post arrive to distract you.

The same principles apply to weekly planning. You may prefer to start your week by planning it on Monday morning, or wind down for the weekend by doing it on Friday afternoon. Whichever you prefer, you should try to produce an outline plan at least a week in advance, especially if you have a major task to tackle.

Don't forget to take your monthly cycle into consideration and plan around it. If you suffer from two days of pre-menstrual short-temper, allocate those days to undemanding routine tasks and do the difficult or stressful jobs when you are in a better state to cope with them. If you don't already know it, find out your daily cycle and allocate alert times to difficult jobs and dull times to coffee breaks. (If dull times don't respond to short breaks and changes of activity, ask yourself if your eating habits are meeting your body's blood sugar needs or if you are getting enough sleep.)

All of which is fine as long as you can keep firm control of your own time. Unfortunately, a large part of any business woman's time is commanded by other people and it is not always easy to sort out priorities. One way to do this is by the 'who pays for lunch?' rule, which is that the person who stands to gain most pays. It's a version of 'What's in it for him, what's in it for me?' If you cannot see any benefit, immediate or future, in whatever it is they want you to do, it gets a 'Z' priority.

You must also learn to say 'I'm sorry, I'm busy' to friends who pay social calls during working hours. This is a major hazard when you work at home. People tend to assume that if you are at home during the day, you are doing the housewife bit and will be delighted to be interrupted. You will be especially prone to this if your work is such that you can do it in casual clothes, and it may help to nip it in the bud if you dress in a businesslike fashion. This is not such a bad idea anyway, as it can be your signal to yourself that work should commence. You will also be less tempted to get involved in domestic chores that catch your eye if you are in smart clothes.

Quite apart from the inability to say 'not now', many of the major time-wasters are self-generated. Procrastination is probably the worst, especially where big jobs are concerned. The more important and complex the job, the greater the fear of failure. So instead of spending several chunks of time telling yourself 'I'll start it tomorrow' why not split it up into a series of little jobs which could at least be started in the same chunks of time? Don't allow yourself to rationalise putting off starting by thinking you'll be fresher tomorrow, or have a big block of time free, or just spend the rest of today clearing your desk so you'll have no distractions tomorrow. If you find yourself thinking along these lines, just stop it and tell the truth – 'I'm wasting time.'

Anyway, why put yourself through the agony of thinking about this horrid job and not getting any of the benefits of getting it done? That way lie ulcers and other stress-related diseases. We all know that dreaded jobs are never as bad as we thought when we do get around to them, so why make such a fuss? Or do you get a kick out of narrowly beating deadlines? Fine – but what are you going to do when flu strikes the day before the deadline and you haven't even started?

Inability to make decisions is also a dreadful waste of your time. Like any other activity, decision-making becomes easier with practice. Write down the problem and list the alternatives. If there is no obvious best solution, ask yourself 'What's the worst that could happen if I'm wrong?' about each alternative and choose the one with the least frightful consequences. Then debrief yourself when you have seen the results and consider why you were right or why you were wrong. Remember, there are only two choices where decisions are concerned – the right one or the wrong one.

Another major time-waster is a lack of organisation. If you know where things are you will not waste your time searching for them. Mother's rule 'don't put it down, put it away!' applies in the office just as much as it does at home. I have heard it suggested that an untidy environment leads to tiredness, on the basis that you actually expend energy by being irritated by the mess. In the long run, the cost of filing equipment will be less than the cost of your time.

Perhaps one ought to say 'Don't put it down, deal with it and put it away.' The only pieces of paper that should go into a 'Pending' tray are the ones where you are waiting for a response from someone before you can complete the job. Everything else should be dealt with or binned.

You can save a lot of time by brushing up your telephone technique, especially when you instigate the call. The basic rules are to keep it short and keep to the point. Both are easier to achieve if you have any papers you might need in front of you and make notes of what you need to say. It means you don't forget anything crucial, and it keeps the cost of the call down too. It is not a bad idea to log all your calls and make notes on what is said. I often find telephone conversations are disputed and it stops all arguments if you are able to quote from your notebook. Since you need to make notes on what you want to say and record the answers somewhere, why not do it in a bound notebook?

You will find, once you start on these time-management techniques, that they become a way of life. Your first consideration in all situations becomes 'is this the best use of my time?' It may not be too easy to mesh your priorities with those of the people you live with, but you must keep at it until you arrive at a workable agreement.

We seem to have allowed the world to persuade us that nothing short of perfection is good enough. You can be a business woman if you want, but you must also be the perfect wife, mother, lover, hostess and housekeeper. Which gives you four options – do it all and run yourself into an early grave in the process; neglect bits and feel guilty about them; kick the others into doing their share; or sit down and reset the family priorities. I assume that you have managed to persuade them that it is a good idea for you to run a business. If not, you'd better sit down and talk that out straight away, or you are in line for some soul-destroying friction.

There are a couple of facts you should keep in mind during that discussion. Assuming that you are over eighteen and have British nationality, you are your own woman. Your body and your possessions belong to you. (A fair chunk of the marital possessions are also yours under the current divorce laws.) You do not have to have permission from your husband or family to run your own business or your own bank accounts, and if they don't like it, short of getting you certified insane, there is not a damn thing they can actually do to stop you doing it. Mind you, they can make your life hell while you are doing it, but you can do the same to them.

That is quite enough of that sort of aggressive nonsense. But the facts remain. The practicalities of continuing to live together on civilised terms usually require compromise, on all sides, and the point at issue here is really whether your new venture is going to inconvenience your family. A little inconvenience never did anybody any harm, particularly if they can be made to see the benefits that will follow. Would your husband and childen rather live in an immaculate house run by a frustrated, bored, boring house-wife, or in a slightly scruffy house with a happy fulfilled lady? I'm afraid the slightly scruffy house is almost obliga-tory until you are making enough to pay to have it done.

Do remember that it is you who lives there, not your mother-in-law. If she really feels the place should be immaculate, maybe she would like to keep it that way herself. After all, why pay an outsider when you could keep it in the family? The only fair arrangement is that since all habitees contribute to dirtying the place, all should help to clean it. Even children, as soon as they are old enough, should look after their own personal space and items, unless a trade-off can be arranged.

Plan the environment itself to be trouble-free. Pale car-pets need constant attention to stay pale. Ornaments need constant dusting. It is possible to live graciously without them. Dark-coloured baths are a menace, especially if you live in a hard-water area. Beds with sheets and blankets take longer to make than beds with duvets, but tall beds with coverlets that hang down to the floor are a wonderful place to hide clutter in an emergency.

Learn to think like that when you are furnishing and you will make your life much easier. Learn to carry things in both hands when leaving a room and you will save two trips. Better still, and especially where food is concerned, get a trolley and do it all in one trip. If at all possible, have your washing machine and tumble drier in the bathroom, so dirty clothes can be taken off bodies and put straight into the machine.

Spend money on good kitchen equipment. Go for maximum

automation and minimum care. Buy non-stick saucepans, food processors, slow cookers, kettles and ovens that switch themselves off, electric plugs with on/off timers built in, a big deep-freeze and a microwave oven.

Then learn the cooking techniques to make the most of them. Don't just cook enough for one meal, make a batch and freeze some. Freeze food in plastic or waxed paper containers rather than foil so the whole thing can go in the microwave. Don't shop more than once a week, less if you have a big enough freezer. Buy ready prepared vegetables and meat so you just have to dump it all in the crock-pot and switch on before you leave in the morning. Give some thought to it all and let your head relieve you of slaving over a hot stove at the end of a busy day.

Teach your children to cook as soon as they are able to do so safely, boys as well as girls – you don't want to be responsible for lumbering some unfortunate girl with looking after your son all his life. Teach them to do other domestic chores and make sure they do their share. You do not do children any favours by letting them grow up without learning that they have to work for what they want.

Teach them to think for themselves. Don't tell them your decisions, consult them when there are decisions to be made. If they are part of the decision-making process, they will be proud to carry out their share of the work. They will also learn to accept as totally natural the fact that you have a business to run and even feel sorry for their friends whose mum stays home all day.

If you cannot be around when your children come home from school, make sure there is someone to meet them. Have set tasks to be performed – left to their own devices they can soon get bored and boredom leads to mischief. Make sure you have someone to call on when emergencies occur. You dare not cancel important business meetings at short notice, so make sure you stay on good terms with Mother-in-Law. You may need her for sickroom duty.

Do look after yourself properly. Get plenty of exercise and sleep. Eat properly, even if you are out on the road selling. Adjust your liquid intake so you don't have to keep dashing to the loo all day or, worse, have to ask if you can use your customer's.

Above all, make time for relaxation. Try to have a whole day at weekends and at least half an hour each day when you do not think about work. Have a warm bath or lie down in a dim room. Breathe deeply and slowly and empty your mind of all its cares. If any stressful thoughts intrude, visualise them written down on a piece of paper and mentally tear up the paper and throw it away. Another technique is to tense your whole body, then relax it, joint by joint, starting at your toes and working up. Take a deep breath at each joint relaxation.

Breathing is an essential part of all relaxation techniques. There are many routines, but I find this one works for me. Breathing both in and out through the nose, pull in your stomach, flatten your diaphragm and raise your ribcage as you breathe in, then reverse the procedure as you breathe out. The whole thing is like a wave advancing and receding. As you breathe, you count, and the four actions of breathing in, holding the breath in, breathing out and holding the breath out, must all take the same length of time. As you practise you will be able to lengthen the times and this is part of the object of the exercise. Your count of 1,2,3,4 will extend to 5,10,15,20. Don't be in any hurry over this, it could take weeks to get that far. It doesn't matter if you don't. What does matter is the rhythm.

If you are unable to relax on your own, join a class in yoga, transcendental meditation or whatever is available locally. You will find that they all rely heavily on breathing exercises and you must keep looking until you find one that suits you. Don't write them off as 'cranky' – they work. But you have to give them a good length of time. There is no such thing as instant relaxation and it may be some months before you begin to reap the benefits.

Don't tell yourself you haven't got time to relax. If you don't do it voluntarily, you might have it forced on you by illness. You just can't afford to be ill, not if you want your business to succeed.

10 Staff

Sooner or later you will find there is more to do than you can cope with on your own and you will be faced with the necessity of taking on employees. It is a big step to have to pay wages and have the additional responsibility of an employee. Not least of all the worries is that of finding the right person. It is not a good idea to employ friends, as it will be very embarrassing if they turn out to be useless. The cheapest way to find staff is at your local Job Centre – it's free! They are very helpful, will tell you if you are eligible for subsidised youngsters, and if you need someone with a special skill, will pass your needs on to other areas.

Employment agencies will be delighted to help and will probably offer to supply you with temps until they have found you someone permanent. This is hardly surprising, as it is very lucrative for them – so much so that it may impair their motivation in finding the permanent person. Their fee for the latter is based on a percentage of the annual salary.

The alternative is to advertise in your local paper. You do not need a big display advert unless you are looking for someone to take a lot of responsibility. Suitable candidates for that sort of job do not read the other little ads unless they are desperate, which means they are not really that suitable. Don't forget that professional headhunters will never touch anybody with what they see as the incurable disease of redundancy.

People who do low-paid or menial jobs like paper-hanging or cleaning tend to move around a lot, so do not expect them to stay with you for ever. Don't expect them to be as keen on it all as you are, either – they mostly feel a job is just a job and a means of getting money.

In a retail situation, you need someone with a sunny disposition, for there is nothing more off-putting to customers than surly shop assistants. A smile and a friendly greeting will do more to bring the customers back again than bargain prices. A smart appearance helps too, so although jeans are perfectly acceptable in many shops, do insist that they are clean and topped by a neat shirt or jumper. Loose garments are likely to catch on various portions of your stock with disastrous results.

The other thing one has to consider these days is that an increasing number of people are non-smokers and find the smell of cigarettes offensive. It lingers on clothing and you don't want your stock to smell of tobacco smoke. You may not want to stipulate that staff do not smoke at all, but you should insist that they do not do so in the shop – nor in the stock room if you have one, because of the fire risk. Something in the region of a third of all shop fires are caused by smoking.

For various reasons connected with current employment law, you might be wise to employ part-time rather than full-time staff. Middle-aged ladies are the best of all, for not only do they tend to have their own transport, they are usually sensible and reliable. They are unlikely to get pregnant, thus involving you in that bit of the legislation, nor will they get together in corners and giggle about their boyfriends.

One other way you might be able to avoid some of the legislation is to split your business into two or more limited companies, the point being that much of the legislation relates only to businesses with four or more employees. This legislation is generally referred to as 'employment protection' but it encompasses a number of different Acts. The legislation tends to change with different governments, but it boils down to the fact that you have to be careful about sacking anyone after they have been with you for twenty-six weeks (this does not apply to certain part-timers).

You must give a contract of employment to each member of staff, listing conditions of employment, hours to be worked, holiday entitlements, salary and periods of notice for ceasing the employment. The easiest method of dealing with this is to set it out in a letter with two copies, requiring the employee to sign one copy as agreed and return it to you for your files.

Employees who consider they have been unfairly dismissed can take you to an industrial tribunal, where you may be ordered to reinstate them, or pay them compensation. Even if you win the tribunal hearing, it will take a great deal of your time and horrendous legal costs. If the employee has been with you for fewer than twenty-six weeks, is a part-timer working less than twenty-one hours per week, is a close relative of yours or is over retiring age, these provisions do not apply. Nor do they apply if you have fewer than four employees.

Employment legislation also covers the employee's right to belong to a trade union or professional association, and to maternity leave, pay while on such leave and the right to return to her job after confinement.

The Equal Pay Act says that employees doing similar work must be paid equally, regardless of sex. The Race Relations Act says you may not discriminate because of race or colour, and the Sex Discrimination Act says you may not discriminate between male and female employees when recruiting, training or promoting employees unless there is a 'genuine occupational qualification' (such as requiring a male employee to assist male customers in the fitting-room) or unless you have fewer than five employees.

The Health and Safety at Work Act says that employers

have a duty to provide and maintain safe machinery and systems of work for their employees, to provide safe handling and storage of potentially dangerous substances, to provide safety information, training and supervision, to take proper care of the working environment and to provide adequate and safe access and egress to working areas. All these provisions also apply to non-employed visitors (e.g. delivery drivers) and there are Health and Safety at Work inspectors who have the power to enter your premises and ensure you are complying with the Act. Obviously, most of these provisions were laid down to protect factory workers, but they can apply to shops as well.

With all your staff, you must operate the PAYE scheme when calculating their wages. The local Inland Revenue office will provide you with all the necessary documentation (ask for their leaflet IR53) and show you how to operate it. Basically it consists of deduction tables for tax and social security contributions, and a record card for each employee. Doing this is another of those tasks that seem frighteningly complex in the abstract, but are simple when you actually do them. You can get some kits from stationers to help or, as I mentioned before, your accountant will do it for you.

You have to pay sick pay to employees for up to eight weeks' sickness in a year. As always, there are exceptions (and a complex formula for working out the payments) but the main exception of interest is that of employees who earn less than the amount at which they have to pay National Insurance.

You must carry 'employers' liability' insurance, which covers unsafe working conditions or equipment, accidents to staff while they are working, and injuries caused by your negligence. You must prove you have this insurance by displaying a valid certificate in a prominent place.

You will also have to comply with the provisions of the Offices, Shops and Railway Premises Act and the Shops Act. These relate to working conditions for employees. The main provisions of the Shops Act relate to the hours a person may work without a break and the length of that break (this does not apply to members of your own family). The Offices, Shops and Railway Premises Act lays down conditions on cleanliness, reasonable temperatures (basically 16°C or 60°F and you must provide a thermometer in a conspicuous place), ventilation, lighting, toilets and washing facilities, seating, accommodation for clothing, fire precautions and first aid facilities – and many other conditions. Failure to comply with these Acts can lead to an inspector closing your premises.

If your head is reeling from all this, and its potentially expensive implications, you will probably be relieved to know that you can get insurance cover to help you with legal costs and awards against you. Called 'employer's protection' cover, it is available from most insurance brokers.

You can, as I mentioned above, avoid much of this hassle by employing only members of your family. What you cannot avoid is National Insurance contributions. Anyone who works and whose remuneration is above a certain level (this changes each year with the Budget) must pay these contributions. In the case of employees, you must deduct these contributions from their wages and, after adding your 'employer's' contribution, must remit these sums regularly to the DHSS, via the Income Tax offices. Income Tax must also be deducted from the wages, and these two amounts are added together and paid in one cheque to the Inland Revenue.

When it comes to working out how much to pay as wages, you should first find out what is considered to be the norm for the job. Most of your potential employees will know very well what the going rate is and won't be impressed if you deviate too far from that in either direction. Too much and they'll know you are a sucker who can be taken advantage of; too little and they'll turn you down, or maybe you'll find the truth of the old saying 'All you get for peanuts is monkeys.'

Some naughty employers come to arrangements with their staff about paying some of the wages in 'under the counter' cash. If you are thus tempted, let me just point out that this money effectively comes from your after-tax pocket, unless you can account for it some other way. Perhaps you were thinking of using some of that undeclared income? Well, all I can say is that you need to have a very good memory and a very good command of book-keeping to indulge safely in this sort of thing. Your accountant won't be too keen either. If he is jealous of his professional status he will refuse to have anything to do with you at all; if he isn't, he'll charge you extra for keeping it quiet. Honesty is best and safest in the long run.

One thing you will have to give some thought to, when you first acquire staff, is your leadership style. You have a choice of two basic styles – autocratic or democratic. These are known in management training circles as Theory X and Theory Y. Theory X assumes that people don't want to work at all and must be made to. To get them to do anything, they must be ordered, threatened and closely controlled. They have no ambition, don't want responsibility and can only be reached by bribery through the wage packet. Theory Y assumes that working is as natural an activity as playing or resting, that people naturally want to produce good results, and that they gain satisfaction from using their ingenuity in solving problems.

You will probably have a strong inclination one way or

the other already. So will your staff. You will not get a good response from Theory Y people if you apply Theory X. Sooner or later they will all leave and you will have to replace them, which will soon prove expensive in advertising, agency fees and time. But whether you take the autocratic route and tell your staff what to do, soften it by explaining why, or consult them before deciding, they must clearly understand that you have the final say.

Use the tone of your voice and your body language to help establish your authority. Stand up straight, look them in the eye and make firm statements: 'I want you to do this' or 'Will you please do that' – and if you do not get an immediate response, add 'Now!' even more firmly. I always find it helps to mentally practise being Lady Bracknell (in *The Importance of Being Earnest*) saying 'A *handbag*?' Maintain a distance between yourself and your staff, particularly if they have never worked for a woman before. You will not get their respect if you try to be 'one of the lads'.

If you have real problems, you will have to consider giving them the sack. Your credibility will not survive if you do not and you do not have time to waste on anyone who is not pulling their weight or is contaminating the work environment with uncooperative attitudes. Firing people is absolute hell. It is a task that everybody hates, but sometimes it must be done. There is a set routine that has to be gone through to comply with the Employment Protection Act of warnings, both verbal and written, but it all comes down to the final crunch in the end. You have to get the person in front of you and tell them 'You're fired.'

Make it easier for yourself by preparation. People who have to do it a lot say you should psych yourself up by finding something personal you dislike – their clothes, habits, political opinions or something nasty they said to or about you. Don't mention any of it to them though, or they will drag you to an Industrial Tribunal. The purpose of the exercise is to harden yourself against them. All you do need to say is something like 'You have been warned already that your work is not up to the required standard and given a chance to improve it. You have not done so. I am not prepared to keep you on my staff any longer.'

It rarely comes to such a drastic situation, but there will be many occasions when you will have to issue a reprimand or criticise a piece of work. General whip-cracking is quite easy. If they are getting noisy or boisterous when there is nothing much to do, you should say something like 'Keep the noise-level down, please' or 'Calm down, you are supposed to be working' – both of which imply you don't really mind. If they have got work to do, 'Settle down now' is a useful phrase.

Criticism of an individual's work should always be done in private. It is the work you are criticising, not the person, and you must not damage their dignity. Adopt the approach that this is a valuable person who happens to have produced a poor piece of work, as in 'You've made a lot of mistakes this week' not 'Your work is deteriorating.' Don't tear the whole thing apart, just point out the specific items that displease you and why. Don't get involved in explanations or excuses. All you are concerned with is the fact that the piece of work is sub-standard. Don't go on about it. Don't bring up any other old grievances. When you have said your piece about it, let that be the end of the matter. To avoid being totally negative, find something in their work you can praise so they can depart on a high note.

Do your praising in public. People like to feel they are valued, and they like it even more if everyone knows it. Keep an eye open for specific things you can praise and say why you like them. Reward them, even if it's only with cake at tea-time. If you don't tell people when you are pleased, they will not know what pleases you, nor how to please you. They can't know they've got it right if you don't say so, any more than they can know what you want if you don't tell them clearly in the first place. Remember the mnemonic KISS – Keep It Simple, Stupid!

There are many work situations where a task has to be performed in a certain way because that is the way the customers like it, or because it is the only way it can be done. These tasks tend to be the ones done at a low level, or those done for an official purpose, such as filling in the VAT return. Teaching such 'mechanical' tasks to one who has never encountered them is a comparatively simple matter. All that is needed is to explain the steps of the task and the fact that it must be done thus and so. If it is done like that, it is right and good. If not, it is wrong and bad. Simple. But more complex and open-ended tasks involve examining the situation, considering alternatives and recommending one of them for action. The situation is less one of instructing than briefing.

Assuming the quality of work is acceptable, the most common disciplinary problem is that of lateness. The first thing you must do is to keep a detailed log of comings and goings. The confrontation, when you are ready for it, must include recorded and accurate facts, for the standard first line of defence in such cases is denial. Once the facts have been accepted as accurate, the second line of defence is inevitably a variation of 'I can't help it'. Your response should be to utilise your standard criticism routine. 'Your general performance is good, but in this respect it is poor. You must learn to do better. I cannot tolerate continued lateness.'

You should then put on your counselling hat and examine the circumstances that cause the bad time-keeping. Whether the problem is family demands, a social life that involves late nights and inadequate sleep, or a metabolism that takes a long time to get going, it inevitably boils down to failure to recognise that it is possible to control your life instead of drifting with the tide. Tempting though it may be to point out that the answer is to go to bed earlier and get up earlier, that is not enough. You need to provide help by discussing and drawing up a specific plan of action. If it works, apply praise. If it doesn't it's back to the drawing-board to revise the plan for another try before applying the big stick. You will not aid your arguments by arriving halfway through the morning yourself.

This will not be the only occasion when you have to adopt a counselling role. Your staff may bring you their personal problems as well as work ones. While you should not necessarily encourage this, you should not reject it. Just be very careful what advice you give. Remember that you are only hearing one side of the story and you should not make value judgements without all the facts. Try not to get involved; that is not the best use of your time. Actually, you will rarely have to, as what is normally needed is a sympathetic but impartial ear. More often than not, having to explain a personal problem lucidly to someone is enough to straighten it out in people's minds and show them what to do. So your role here is that of a sounding-board. The only situation where you may need to take some action is when the problem involves another member of staff.

Even without problems, if you are not working alongside them, you should check on your staff at least once a day. Then you will know if they need any help. Better still, you should spend long enough with them at the beginning of each day to see if anyone is feeling low. Even without intruding into their private life you can give a boost to their day by greeting them brightly and spending a little time with them.

It does no harm to de-brief people immediately after a major project. Then any problems will be fresh in their minds. But it should also be done at regular intervals to evaluate the way you operate. A good team as an entity will be greater than the sum of its component parts. You will get so used to working with each other that you will develop a communication system that will be practically telepathic.

But never forget that a team is made up of individuals. To get the best out of them you must get to know them, for if you do not know how they tick you cannot know how best to apply pressure or assistance when it is needed. If you have a large staff you will need to cultivate a good memory, for at the very least you must remember where each person lives, the name of their spouse and their main hobby. If your memory is poor, keep a prompt sheet on each person and consult it before they come into your office. Make sure you remember birthdays in time to buy a card. Don't keep a stock of cards in your desk – someone is sure to find out and that negates the value of the whole thing.

These personal details are your key to the conversations which will unlock your staff's personalities. Some will be straight-talkers who mean what they say and do what they say. Others are devious, never give a straight answer and spend half their time trying to work out what you meant by what you said. Some think they can fast-talk their way out of trouble and some are so far away in their heads all the time that they hardly talk at all. Some need only the outline of an idea and will be offended if you try to explain the details, while others need to have the whole thing explained laboriously several times and still go away muttering 'I don't understand.'

Some are larks, best in the morning, and others are owls who barely function at all before tea-time. It's no good trying to explain a new concept to them first thing in the morning. Some are meticulously precise and others reckon that some mud will stick to the wall if they throw enough of it. You will need to vary your delivery for each one, just as you do when you are selling.

But they all have their strengths and weaknesses. It is your responsibility to develop the one and modify the other. Most people can be encouraged to develop by the simple fact that someone believes they can do so. They need opportunities to show their potential and earn recognition for good work. Show them that you will applaud attempts at improvement, successful or not, and you will remove the fear of failure and encourage them to try again until they do succeed. One of the best ways to do this is to give them a task that they have to do all on their own – and let them do it. You'll need to brief them thoroughly, but once the task is given, you must not see it again until it is completed. Don't tell them how to do it, just what you want done. Let them work it out for themselves. It doesn't matter if they do it differently from the way you would, as long as the result is right.

And don't just hand over the boring jobs. People will not develop without challenges. You should look at every job that comes your way and ask yourself which of your staff can do it, not wonder when you are going to find the time to do it yourself.

11 Expansion

If your business is in any way successful, it is bound to grow. Indeed, it must, for in this inflationary age if you do not grow you are actually going backwards. In business, as in banking, a plateau is abhorrent.

At the very least your turnover should increase at the same percentage rate as the commodities around you, assuming that your profit margin remains constant. If that profit margin is dropping, you have reached saturation point, which in this context means not that everybody who might want a widget has one, but that the cost of selling extra widgets is actually more than the profit on them. You can only go so far without having to make some policy decisions on where you want to go next. The first of these is whether you really want the business to get that much bigger, instead of just keeping pace with inflation, or whether you like things the way they are now.

One consideration that does not affect men in this situation as much as it does women is the business of having babies. We are told that we have a 'biological time-bomb' ticking away inside us that urges us to breed. It doesn't affect all of us, for reasons ranging from disinclination to advanced age, but for those of us who do want to start a family the problem exists.

Can you run your business while you are pregnant? Will your protruding tummy physically impede you, or be off-putting to the people you are dealing with? How long will you have to have off work to give birth? How are you going to cope with the baby? Leave it with someone else all day – are you *sure* you want to do that? When you've thought your way through that lot and discussed it with your partner (it's his baby too, and he should have a say in its upbringing) you may come to the conclusion that you should sell your business and start another when you've finished being maternal.

Your children may on the other hand be one of the reasons you do want to expand, to build something for their future. You may think bigger is safer, you may get a lot of satisfaction from seeing your brain-child prosper, or you may just feel that now you know what you're doing it is time you began to reap some real benefit from it. Or it may be that in the process of doing whatever it is you do, you have become aware of something else that needs doing. Your dress-shop customers may tell you that there is nowhere in town to buy decent shoes, or sexy lingerie, and you could profitably open up a new shop or department to fill that need.

Your customers may also complain that there isn't a decent butcher in town, but unless it happens that you have a butcher in the family it would not be a good idea to go into that business. The gap between dresses and meat is too large and you will be permanently torn between the two. That is the danger of diversification – the temptation to go off at unrelated tangents. You must have seen, as I have, people who waste their energy by running frantically in several different directions. Unless your business is management consultancy, or another type of enterprise where you have to get involved in different kinds of businesses, stick to what you know, decide where you want to go, and go there – in a straight line.

You may feel at this point that you need some assistance in charting your plan of action. As always, there will be plenty of organisations willing to take your money in return for nebulous benefits. One area where this is particularly prevalent at the moment is conferences and seminars. The fees for these can be exorbitant, and despite some of them having 'household name' speakers, the content can only be generalised, for they want to attract as many paying 'delegates' as possible. Apart from the general run of these, which are not specifically aimed at women, there is now the 'women in management/women in business' bandwagon. If you want to attend these functions, first find out as much detail as you can about the content to evaluate the likely benefit. One of the major benefits is making business contacts, so ask who the other delegates are – you may find half of them are journalists looking for a story which is unlikely to include a useful plug for your business.

Many colleges run reasonably priced courses, both long and short, as do the Manpower Services Commission, although these tend to be attended mostly by men. If you find that idea intimidating, the Pepperell Unit of The Industrial Society run excellent courses for women. I have attended some of these myself and can recommend them. But these will still be rather generalised, although you will be able to ask detailed questions. For really personalised assistance, don't forget the Small Firms Service and its free counselling sessions.

What the experts will all ask is whether you are sure you are doing the best you can with what you already have. Expansion will inevitably cost money and if you can squeeze a bit more profit out of what you are already doing, so much the better. You may be able to raise your prices without upsetting your customers, but you need to do some sums to work out the critical point. If you buy widgets at £1 each and you sell 100 a week at £2, you've made £100. If you put the price up to £3, as long as you sell 50 you haven't lost anything and if you sell more than 50 you're laughing. At £2.50, you've got to sell 67 to make your £100. It depends, of course, on your product/service and on whether your customers are one-offs or regulars, but the way to find out what the market will bear is to ease your prices up gradually until you reach the sales drop-off point.

Another way of tackling this is to reduce the content of the product while keeping the price static. This does not just apply in such situations as the ever-diminishing bar of chocolate, but also in a service where you might exclude the ancillaries (such as typing the report) from your price for the job.

Do you have any customers who are more trouble than they are worth? Don't fall into the trap of assuming that big customers are always a good thing. They tend to be picky about quality, want special attention, and they are not necessarily that prompt when it comes to paying. You may do better without them, especially if they are the sort that pull nasty tricks if they get you into the position of being dependant on them.

I have heard from several sources of one horsey-goods wholesaler in America who took advantage of a series of saddlery manufacturers here. He would place a small order, then a bigger one, and another even bigger, all of which were accepted and paid for without problems. Then he would suggest that at a slightly lower price he would buy all his saddles from that firm – several thousand a year. With stars in their eyes, they would sign the contract, enlarge their factories, take on more staff and start to send the shipments across. Then they found that an increasing number of the saddles were being designated 'sub-standard' on arrival. They were offered the options of accepting a ridiculously low price for them, or paying the freight costs to have them returned. A couple of companies even went into liquidation because of it.

The other side of putting your prices up is to bring your

costs down. You need to examine each aspect of your operation, rather as you did when you were looking for time-savers. Look at your raw materials, processes, advertising, premises, staff – especially staff. I don't mean that you should fire people, but if they do leave can they be replaced with someone cheaper? I know of many businesses, including one famous shop in London, which keep a small hard core of mature long-term staff and fill the gaps with cheap youngsters who are fired just before they reach the twenty-six week deadline.

Another thought is new markets. If you are trading on a small localised scale, the next step is the comparatively simple one of opening another shop or office in another location. All you do here is repeat the exercises you did for your first place, but then you come up against a snag. Who is going to run the second place? Will they care enough to do it the way you want them to? Will they dip their fingers in the till? The worst situation of all is when you are still tied to your first outlet, for then they know where you will be all the time. You would do better to put managers in both and flit between the two, for then neither will know when you are going to be with them.

The other end of the 'new market' scale is exporting. It is not a game for bright-eyed bushy-tailed novices. If you don't have good experience of it already, in which case you don't need me to tell you how to go about it, you should start with our old friend the Small Firms Service, or the British Overseas Trade Board. The easiest way to start is by selling your goods to an export house, which is little different to an ordinary wholesale customer, or to a UK buying house for foreign customers.

Maybe you have a new product in mind. Are you sure it will sell? Consider where you will get it from and whether you should abandon an existing line in its favour. If you are going to make it, what will you need in order to do so and where are you going to get it from?

If it is a brilliant new idea of your own, have you done all that is necessary to protect it? There is a tendency for the innocent to say, 'Oh, I will get it patented!' without any idea of the costs or complications of the process. Patents only apply to actual objects, and they must be clearly definable as unique. There are some 20 million items already patented, and your idea must be different from any other to be granted a patent. Exhaustive searches through the registers must be carried out, which takes a long time, and at the end of it, if your widget is truly unique, the patent granted will only cover you for a certain time and certain countries. If you want world coverage, you have to go through the process in virtually each country.

You can also register designs and trade marks by going through similar processes. You would do best to do whichever is appropriate through a patent agent. They will advise you on whether your idea is registrable, take over the registration process (for a fee of course), help you get some insurance to pay for the legal costs of suing infringers, and put you in touch with buyers if you don't want to develop and market your idea yourself. You do this either by selling your rights outright, or by selling a 'licence'.

This latter is the basis of the franchise system, which is probably the least painful method of expansion. You make your money while others take the day-to-day risks, though of course you do have an on-going involvement. At the very least you must ensure that your standards are maintained or the image and thus the value of your format will go downhill.

You get your money from various areas of the operation – a 'joining' fee on signing the contract, an annual 'royalty' for the use of your name and format (often based on a percentage of takings), the sale of supplies (both stationery and products or raw materials), commissions from various sources ranging from advertising agencies through finance houses to shop-fitters, and a fee for management services. On an on-going basis, it costs you staff or time for negotiating, evaluating, general 'setting-up assistance' and training; your subscription to the British Franchise Association; and advertising costs for attracting new franchisees. To set it up you will have to organise a comprehensive operating manual, various items of raw materials, a distribution system for these, a good contract (the BFA will help you with this) and your own administration system.

Apart from keeping standards up, the main problems you will encounter will be the ones which come in any business situation: conflicts of personality, people who decide they don't need you any more, and people who think you need them so desperately that you will reduce your price. This is not a good idea, even when you start. You can give your ideas (or your goods) away to anyone – but if it's worth having, it's worth paying for.

But if you don't want anyone else to have a slice of your action and you are set on a major expansion, you must prepare yourself for a quantum leap. You are going to need some high-level staff to help you with all the aspects of your business and you are going to have to learn to loosen your hold on the reins a little. You will no longer be able to oversee every little detail and you mustn't even try. You hire quality senior people because you need their expertise and they will expect to be left in peace to use it.

I would suggest that the first person you hire is a properly qualified company secretary. By properly qualified, I mean a member of the Institute of Chartered Secretaries and Administrators. Many company secretaries are accountants or solicitors, but their training does not encompass quite the same spectrum of skills as the ICSA. Apart from company law, they cover most aspects of business law, accountancy, data processing and personnel management, all of which you are going to need.

As you get bigger, you may need specialists in these and other fields. The best use of your time now is in strategic planning and overseeing, not learning the basic rules of survival in specialist fields. The first set of specialists you must consult are the ones with expertise in expansion – either management consultants or one of the big national firms of accountants. Apart from being able to guide you through the maze of subsidies, grants and tax credits I mentioned before (and you must be prepared to shift most of your operation geographically to get the best of these) they will help you work out who and what you need in the way of second-rank management. They will help you draw up detailed job specifications and tell you the appropriate salaries to offer. Since most of them have associated recruitment agencies or headhunters within their operations, they will also be able to help you actually find the right people.

They will also help you get the big chunk of money you will inevitably need. You are bound to need better and/or bigger premises, a real computer (not just a series of desktop machines) with all that that implies, possibly new machinery or bigger stocks, more staff, and so on. It all takes money.

The first task, if you are not already operating as a limited company, is to set one up. Even if you are already incorporated, you must ensure that the format is suitable. The 'off-the-shelf' companies I mentioned before tend to have only 100 £1 shares, and that is not appropriate in this situation. You do not have to start or buy a new company, all that is needed is to restructure the one you have, usually by declaring a new issue of shares. Nobody has to put up any money for these at this stage and they do not have to be allocated to anyone, but they must be available if needed. Many sources of venture capital want a substantial chunk of your company's equity (as well as interest) for their money. A lot of them will also want to put one of their people in a strategic position on your board of directors.

Where do you actually go for the money? As before, you start with your own bank. Talk to your branch manager, who will pass you on to the appropriate specialist department. If they don't like the idea, they will probably pass you on to ICFC (Industrial and Commercial Finance Corporation Ltd) which is actually owned by the clearing banks and the Bank of England. ICFC does not finance start-ups, but is one of the few sources that will lend small amounts for situations that do not merit bank loans, and that does so on a long-term basis.

Most venture capital houses want their money back within five years. They are predominantly run by merchant banks, and they like to keep their money turning over. They like it to be safe, too, and they are not generally keen on service companies without a solid backing of assets. As to which one to approach, you should be guided by your tame expert. Like everyone else, providers of venture capital tend to specialise in certain areas where they have experience. They will all, whoever they are, from a clearing bank to merchant bankers, want a very detailed and formally presented proposal. Some like it to come from you direct, some prefer it to come from one of the leading firms of accountants. The former will nominate one of these firms to investigate you and report back.

Your proposal document must be immaculately presented. It should ideally be bound, or at least presented in a solid cover, with good dividers between the sections. It will

also need an index, an outline summary of its contents, and
appendices of supporting documentation. You should have
several copies prepared as interested lenders will want
more than one. You may need to show it to several lenders
before you find one that will take you on, and although the
'Thanks but no thanks' companies will return it to you, it
may not come back in the pristine condition needed to go
to the next.

Start with a brief history of your business, from its
inception to date. This should include details of structure,
original capital, any past or current loans, and a summary
chart of year-end figures. Balance sheets and profit and loss
accounts for at least three years should be in the appendix.
They will want to see a steady growth, not a picture of
erratic progress.

The order in which the rest of the information is presented is up to you, but I would suggest that most lenders will
want to know about the money next. Tell them how much
you want, why you are having to borrow it and what you
actually intend to spend it on. Vague statements like
'expanding our production' will not do. If it is to be spent on
premises, for instance, state your favoured geographical
location, size of building needed, and cost of this accommodation (with a couple of sample brochures from local
estate agents in the appendix). Tell them how long you want
it for, and prove your ability to repay the capital and the
interest by detailed cash flows over that period.

Tell them what assets you have and prove their worth
with more than one current valuation from independent
sources. Say whether they are already encumbered as
security for other borrowings, and if so, when this will
cease. Since debtors are assets, give some details of your
sales ledger, your bad debt ratios and what controls you
have to reduce them. Don't forget your liabilities, either.

Most of them will be self-explanatory from your cash flow, but if anything needs detailed explanation, give it.

They will want to know who will be looking after their money, so tell them. Provide CV's for yourself and your key managers. Say who reports to whom, who has responsibility for what, and if there is any vital function not covered say so and say what you are doing to fill the gap. Say also whether these crucial people are covered by 'key-man' insurance. (This gives your business a lump sum to recruit and train a replacement if anyone should die.)

Tell them about your product. Give a detailed description in layman's terms (technical data in the appendix for them to pass on to an expert if need be) and add a photograph or drawings if possible. Say if it is protected by patents, trade marks or registered designs, and the scope and duration of this protection. Give some details of your Research and Development department and the manufacturing process.

Say where your production plant is, how big it is, what the workforce consists of, whether it is unionised and, if so, what is its history of industrial action. Say where and how you get your raw materials, what stocks you hold (stated as days' or weeks' supplies) and what contingency plans you have to cover breakdown in supply. Give details of any subcontractors you use and what back-up you have in case they give you trouble.

Say how your product is placed with its competitors, whether its market share is static, increasing or decreasing. Give some details on your competitors and discuss how dangerous they are to your market position.

What are your markets? Are they growing, and at what rate? Who said so, and when? Include market research reports and surveys, stating their source and whether you had them specially prepared. If you have copies of any useful articles from the trade or general press, include them, again showing the date of publication and source.

Discuss any seasonal peaks, your pricing strategy, and how you deal with sales and distribution. Provide charts of the geographical breakdown of your sales and give details of your plans to fill any gaps, or reasons for not doing so. If you have any plans to change the structure of your sales network (e.g. from independent agents to an employed sales force) discuss those and their likely effect on your cash flow. Give some details of your advertising strategy and its costs. Include the agency's campaign proposals if you have one, with copies of any relevant artwork.

Don't forget to include details of any laws or regulations which currently affect you, or which are in the pipeline and will do so in the future. How do they or will they affect your business and how do you cope? Will future legislation involve you in extra cost (e.g. environmental controls) or personnel?

If there is anything I haven't mentioned that you think they ought to know, put that in too. Then wait for the answer. But be patient – it will take several months to evaluate that lot and check it all out.

The time will come when you get beyond the stage of borrowing money and want to join the real big-time by going public. You will probably think of the Unlisted Securities Market. This is run by the Stock Exchange, and its main difference from a full listing is that you do not have to release more than 10 per cent of your equity to the public. (A full listing requires a minimum of 25 per cent.) You have to be sponsored by a stockbroker, although this is frequently arranged by merchant banks. You will be unlikely to find a willing sponsor until your profits are in the region of £250,000 per annum.

The procedures are rigidly controlled by the Stock

Exchange, the Prevention of Fraud (Investments) Act and the Companies Act. For more details, ask for the USM booklet from accountants Touche Ross and Co.

Postscript

I hope you make it that far. It won't be easy, but then nothing worthwhile ever is. On the other hand, the satisfaction of working for yourself and the opportunity to gain financial independence are always worth the effort involved. And like any new activity, the more you do it, the easier it gets.

I have a theory about this, which I call Cliffs and Plateaus. The cliffs are the breakthroughs (like finding a new outlet for your product) and the plateaus are the periods when you consolidate the results of your new discovery (like learning how best to pack and display your product for the new marketplace). Your goal is the top of the mountain, but you have to climb all these cliffs and cross all the plateaus to get there.

When you start out, the cliffs are small and the plateaus wide, but the more you learn about your chosen business and the more useful contacts you make, so you begin to jump up larger cliffs and find the plateaus in between are shorter, until you can step easily up the last gentle incline to the summit.

Just keep your wits about you and remember Macdonald's Maxim – 'It's a hard, cruel world, and a girl must look after herself as best she can – because nobody else will!'

Appendix One
Cash Flow Forecast

	Jan		Feb		Mar		Apl	
	Actual	Budget	Actual	Budget	Actual	Budget	Actual	Bu
Income								
Zero-rated	3804	4000	2900	4000	4680	4000		4
Standard-rated	10,397	9000	9842	9000	5267	4000		4
VAT	1560	1350	1476	1350	790	600		
Total income	15,761	14,350	14,218	14,350	10,737	8600		8
Expenditure								
Stock	5927	6000	4829	6000	7287	6000		6
Wages	1000	1000	1000	1000	1000	1000		1
Rent	1875	1875						1
Rates	100	100						
Electricity	226	200						
Telephone	212	200						
Insurance	876	900						
Motor expenses	278	300	179	200	224	200		
Repairs & maintenance		250			167			
Accountancy								
Security	150	150	150	150	150	150		
Contingencies		100	57	100		100		
General	27	100	119	100	43	100		
Loan Repayments	1300	1300						
Bank Charges	206	100						
VAT	498	500	380	500	502	500		
Total Expenditure	12,675	13,075	6714	8050	9373	8050		1
Month's Balance	3086	1275	7504	6300	1364	550		(
Cumulative Balance (Year)	3086	1275	10,590	7575	11,954	8125		

May	June	J.A.S.	O.N.D.	J.F.M.	A.M.J.	J.A.S.	O.N.D.
...al Budget	Actual Budget	Budget	Budget	Budget	Budget	Budget	Budget
4000	4000	12,000	12,000	13,200	13,200	13,200	13,200
4000	4000	17,000	27,000	25,000	25,000	19,000	39,000
600	600	2550	4050	3750	3750	2850	4500
8600	8600	31,550	43,050	41,950	41,950	35,050	47,700
6000	6000	18,000	31,000	20,000	20,000	20,000	35,000
1000	1000	3000	3000	3300	3300	3300	3300
		1875	1875	1875	1875	1875	1875
		100	100	120	120	120	120
		200	200	250	250	250	250
		200	200	250	250	250	250
		900		1000		1000	
200	200	600	600	800	700	700	700
		250		300		300	
	1200				1400		
150	150	450	450	500	500	500	500
100	100	300	300	300	300	300	300
100	100	300	300	300	300	300	300
		1300	1300	1300	1300	1300	1300
		300	300	350	350	350	350
500	500	1500	4000	1700	1700	1700	3950
8050	9250	29,275	43,625	32,345	32,345	32,245	48,195
550	(650)	2275	(575)	9605	9605	2805	(495)
5450	4800	7075	6500	9605	19,210	22,015	21,520

Notes
1. This cash flow relates to a newly opened shop
   where takings fluctuate seasonally.
2. VAT has been calculated at a standard rate
   of 15 per cent.
3. In the Balance lines, the accounting convention
   of showing minus figures in brackets has been used.

Useful Addresses

British Overseas Trade Board
1 Victoria Street, London SW1H 0ET

British Franchise Association
75a Bell Street, Henley-on-Thames, Oxon

Business in the Community (for list of enterprise agencies)
227a City Road, London EC1V 1LX

Central Office of Information (for statistics)
Hercules Road, London SE1

Deloittes, Haskins and Sells
(Publication Department, for useful booklets)
25 Bread Street, London EC4V 4AJ

Department of Trade and Industry (Small Firms Division)
Ashdown House, 123 Victoria Street, London SW1E 6RB

Equipment Leasing Association
(for booklets and list of leasing companies)
18 Upper Grosvenor Street, London W1

Health and Safety Executive (for booklets on various regulations)
1 Long Lane, London SE1 4PG

ICFC Ltd
91 Waterloo Road, London SE1 8XP

The Industrial Society
(The Pepperell Unit, for training courses)
Robert Hyde House, 48 Bryanston Square,
London W1H 7LN

Institute of Marketing
Moor Hall, Cookham, Berks SL6 9QH

Kompass Publishers
(sales guides and other directories)
Windsor Court, East Grinstead, W. Sussex RH19 1XD

The Mail Order Trader's Association
507 Corn Exchange Building, Fenwick Street,
Liverpool L2 7RA

The Small Business Bureau
(has an advisory service and publishes the bi-monthly
newspaper *small business*)
32 Smith Square, London SW1P 3HH

Touche-Ross and Co
Hill House, 1 Little New Street, London EC4A 3TR

Women's networks: for a complete list write for the booklet
entitled 'Women's Organisations in Great Britain' to the
Women's National Commission, Government Offices,
Great George Street, London SW1. Two of the best that have
come to my attention are: Network, 25 Park Road, London
NW1 6XN and Women in Management, 74 Cottenham Park
Road, London SW20 0TB

Some women experts in raising business finance and in
pensions are:
Mrs A. Brett, 9 Howell Road, Exeter, Devon
Ms R. Caira, 3 Louise Avenue, Forest Grange, Groby, Leics
Mrs D, Nockels, Walnut House, The Street, Ubley, Avon
BS18 6PA
Mrs J. Tame, 1st Floor, Kingsway House, 103 Kingsway,
London WC2

Among the many companies offering financial services,
Hill Samuel Investment Services Ltd (NLA Tower, Addis-
combe Road, Croydon, Surrey) is probably the best, and it
has many women advisers.

Select Bibliography

There are many books on all the aspects of running a small (or large) business. These are some of the better ones I have found.

A to Z of Employment and Safety Law, Peter Chandler (Kogan Page, 1981)

Be Your Own PR Man, Michael Bland (Kogan Page, 1981)

Consumer Law for the Small Business, Patricia Clayton (Kogan Page, 1983)

Everything is Negotiable, Gavin Kennedy (Business Books Ltd, 1982)

How to Buy a Business, Peter Farrell (Kogan Page, 1983)

How to Get Control of Your Time and Your Life, Alan Lakein (Peter H. Wyden, 1973)

How to Start and Run Your Own Shop, P. Levene (Graham and Trotman, 1985)

Law for the Small Business, Patricia Clayton (Kogan Page, 1979)

Megatrends, John Naisbitt (Macdonald Futura, 1984)

The Small Business Guide, Colin Barrow (BBC Publications, 1982)

Taking up a Franchise, Godfrey Golzen, Colin Barrow and Jackie Severn (Kogan Page, 1983)

VAT Made Easy, A. St J. Price (Kogan Page, 1979)

What They Don't Teach You at Harvard Business School, Mark H. McCormack (Collins, 1984)

Index